A NATURA~~~~

BIRDS
OF EGYPT AND THE
MIDDLE EAST

Richard Hoath

JOHN BEAUFOY PUBLISHING

TO GEMMA AND WILLIAM

First published in the United Kingdom in 2021 by John Beaufoy Publishing Ltd
11 Blenheim Court, 316 Woodstock Road, Oxford OX2 7NS, England
www.johnbeaufoy.com

Photo Credits
Front cover: *main image* White-tailed Lapwing © Manjula Mathur. *Bottom row, left to right* Hoopoe © Biswaroop Satpati; Nile Valley Sunbird © Dina Aly; Lesser Spotted Eagle © Bikram Grewal. **Back cover**: Greater Hoopoe Lark © Arpit Deomurari. **Title page**: Greater Painted Snipe © Bikram Grewal. **Contents page**: White-eyed Gull © Dina Aly Hamdy.

Main descriptions: Photographs listed by a page number followed by t (top), b (bottom), l (left), c (centre) or r (right).
Dina Aly & Rafik Khalil 20b, 34t, 37b, 38b, 39t, 51t, 85b, 88t, 108br, 125b, 128b, 142t, 142b, 145b, 147bl, 148b, 155t, 156t; **Dina Aly Hamdy** 29b, 35t, 47bl, 51b, 75b, 76, 83t, 92, 98b, 103b, 147br; **Anand Arya** 48br; **Jem Babbington** 103c; **Garima Bathia** 18t, 23t, 25br, 44t, 89b, 128t, 151bl, 156b; **Dave Barnes** 41bl, 121bl, 124t, 150t; **Siddhesh Bramhankar** 83b; **Raymond de Smet** 30t, 33bl, 36c, 40t, 77tr, 77b, 78br, 87t, 108bl, 119b, 135t, 135bl, 136br, 143tr; **Arpit Deomurari** 60b, 158t; **Nikhil Devasar** 15b, 30b, 54tr, 81t, 104t, 116bl, 136t; **Kintoo Dhawan** 21tl; **Savio Fonseca** 17t, 21b, 22t, 28b, 31b, 34b, 35b, 45b, 50b, 60tl, 62t, 63t, 65t, 66b, 68b, 70b, 73b, 74t, 79b, 80b, 87c, 90t, 91t, 98t, 99t, 99b, 102t, 119t, 140b, 143tl, 146b, 148t, 149t; **Clement M. Francis** 26b, 44b, 52bl, 55t, 84t, 116br, 126bl; **Bikram Grewal** 14t, 14bl, 15t, 16b, 18b, 22b, 23b, 24tr, 24c, 24b, 25tl, 27t, 28t, 29t, 32t, 33t, 36b, 38t, 39b, 40b, 41tl, 42b, 45t, 46tr, 46b, 47br, 48t, 49t, 52t, 52br, 53t, 54tl, 54b, 56b, 58b, 59t, 61t, 61br, 67b, 72b, 77tl, 78t, 79tl, 82b, 84b, 85t, 86t, 86b, 89t, 90b, 94bl, 95, 97t, 100t, 107t, 107b, 109b, 110t, 111tl, 111b, 114t, 114b, 115t, 116cc, 117b, 118b, 120t, 120b, 121t, 122tl, 122b, 123t, 124bl, 124br, 126t, 126br, 127t, 127b, 129t, 130b, 131t, 132t, 133bl, 133br, 134tl, 137t, 139b, 141tl, 141tr, 143b, 144b, 147t, 151tl, 152br, 154t, 154b, 157t, 158b; **H Çaglar Güngor** 14br, 19t, 24tl, 31t, 36t, 41br, 62b, 65b, 70t, 81b, 82t, 88b, 93t, 93b, 94t, 96t, 96b, 105tr, 105b, 106t, 109t, 110bl, 111tr, 112t, 113t, 113b, 121br, 122tr, 129b, 130tr, 133t, 135br, 137br, 145tl, 145tr, 146t, 149b, 152bl, 157b; **Vaidehi Gunjal** 152t; **Stanislav Harvançik** 153; **Mohamed Hazem** 48br; **Neil Hewison** 115b; **Brian James** 94br; **Ashok Kashyap** 97b; **Sunil Kini** 27b, 47t, 49bl, 49br, 57b, 102b, 105tl, 117t, 134b; **Manjula Mathur** 16t, 17b, 19b, 33bl, 42t, 43b, 53b, 55b, 57t, 59b, 60tr, 61bl, 64b, 66t, 67t, 69t, 69b, 71t, 71b, 73t, 116tl, 140t; **David Monticelli** 87b, 123b, 131b, 138b; **Kunan Naik** 32b, 106b; **Mike Pope** 37tr, 41tr, 50t, 78bl, 79tr, 103t, 118t, 130tl, 136bl, 138t, 141br, 144t, 150b; **Huw Roberts/wildlifeuae** 75t; **Biswaroop Satpati** 25bl, 46tl, 58t, 63b, 64t, 101b, 116tr; **Sumit Sen** 37tl, 72t; **Amit Sharma** 68t; **Khushboo Sharma** 20t, 43t, 48bl; **Shutterstock/**Agami Photo Agency 125t, Dervis Kokenek 21tr, Michal Pesata 108t, skapuka 134tr, Txanbelin 56t, valdi9 132b, Vitaly Ilyasov 155b, Vladimir Melnik 25tr, Wolfgang Kruck 74b; **Clive Temple** 26t, 100b, 110br, 136c, 139t, 151tr, 151br; **Rick van der Weijde** 104b, 112b; **Kilian Weixler** 80t, 137bl; **Mike Williams** 91bl, 101t, 141bl.

Great care has been taken to maintain the accuracy of the information contained in this work. However, neither the publishers nor the authors can be held responsible for any consequences arising from the use of the information contained therein.

ISBN 978-1-913679-02-6

Edited by Krystyna Mayer
Designed by Nigel Partridge
Printed and bound in Malaysia by Times Offset (M) Sdn. Bhd.

·CONTENTS·

Introduction

The area covered by this book is Egypt, at the northeasternmost corner of the African continent, and the Middle East. This region is often seen as synonymous with the desert and the popular image of vast tracts of arid dunes. While this may be true of certain areas, such as Arabia's *Rub' al-Khali* or Empty Quarter, and Egypt's Great Sand Sea in the Western Desert, Egypt includes the fertile Nile Delta and Valley, and the wider region includes mountain ranges, rich wetlands, mangroves, and extensive coastal habitat. Moreover, the desert itself is a varied habitat ranging from dune fields to barren *hamada* (rocky plains) and massifs gorged and riddled with wadis that are sometimes richly vegetated. Egypt alone has a species list approaching 500 birds, while the Arabian Peninsula supports a number of endemics, not least in the highlands of southern Arabia and Yemen. Perhaps the great attraction of the region to ornithologists, however, is the twice-yearly spectacle of migration. Each spring, tens of millions of migratory birds head north through the region from local or sub-Saharan wintering grounds to northern breeding quarters, and in the autumn the movement is reversed. For the largest birds, the larger raptors, cranes, storks, pelicans, and so on, the routes are channelled through specific migration hotspots, providing birdwatchers with one of nature's greatest spectacles.

In Egypt, perhaps uniquely, the avifauna has been portrayed with great accuracy on the walls of tombs and temples many thousands of years old that can be visited to this day. Nowhere else in the world can you stand and admire the representation of the falcon-headed god Horus, at Kom Ombo in the Nile Valley, for instance, only to find that a pair of the living bird, the Common Kestrel, is breeding on a masonry ledge in that same temple today.

This guide is ideal not just for the modern birdwatcher but also for the keen amateur visiting the ancient monuments throughout the Nile Valley and Delta, who can marvel at the representations on the tomb walls, then identify the living counterparts that still abound today. On the tomb walls of Mereruka, Ti, and Idut at Saqqara, the birds of the long-drained papyrus swamps of the Valley and Delta can be identified to species level – such is the accuracy of their portrayal. Pied Kingfishers hover over the swamp scenes as they do today over the Nile, while Purple Swamphens, egrets, and herons stalk the reeds. At Beni Hasan, in the tomb of Khnumhotep III, Pintails, Turtle Doves, Hoopoes, Masked and Red-backed Shrikes, and Common Redstarts are all painted in such detail that this book will help in identifying the species not just for the naturalist but for the Egyptologist.

Biogeography of Egypt & the Middle East

Egypt is situated in northeastern Africa and is directly linked to the Middle East through the Sinai Peninsula. That connection today is only breached by the artificial Suez Canal. The Middle East proper, referred to throughout this book as the **Region**, is a much more complex entity in many ways, not least politically, geographically and, of concern here, biologically. Here the Middle East covers Syria, Lebanon, Jordan, Israel and the Occupied Territories, Saudi Arabia, Kuwait, Qatar, Bahrain, United Arab Emirates, Oman, and Yemen (not including the island of Socotra). These diverse countries can be split into distinct subregions.

Egypt today comprises an area of about 1,019,449km^2, of which some 18,000km^2

are in the southeasternmost corner of the country, known as the Sudan Government Administration Area, or Halaib Triangle. The significance of this area is that in biogeographical terms it is not part of the Western Palearctic. The official records of the Egyptian Ornithological Rarities Committee document 466 species from the country, including seven only recorded from the Halaib Triangle. There are no endemic bird species, probably largely due to the artificial borders of the modern state, based on political agreement rather than natural boundaries such as rivers or mountains. While the popular perception of Egypt is that of pyramids and desert, the truth is rather different. Even the desert – and Egypt is widely quoted to be up to 96 per cent desert – is a surprisingly rich and varied habitat.

Egypt has two coastlines. The northern Mediterranean coastline stretches from Sallum in the west on the Libyan border, east to Alexandria, and across the coastal lakes of the northern Nile Delta and farther across north Sinai. The coastal strip, referred to here as the **North Coast** between Sallum and Alexandria, is of particular importance. It is cooler and has higher rainfall than the rest of Egypt, and supports a distinctive flora and fauna. Some species, such as the Barbary Partridge and Dupont's Lark, may be locally extinct due to hunting and habitat destruction but others remain, such as the Common Raven, the rare Houbara Bustard, and the very local Thekla Lark and Red-rumped Wheatear. Farther east the lakes of the northern Delta, such as Maryut, Idku, Burullus, and Manzala, and on farther to Bardawil in northern Sinai, support a rich avifauna hosting large flocks of waterfowl and waders in winter, along with gulls, including Audouin's Gull, and tern species, egrets, and herons, and smaller numbers of Greater Flamingo. On migration, and especially in autumn, these same areas, as the first landfall for birds crossing the Mediterranean heading south, offer fabulous birdwatching opportunities. Sadly, there is a long history of bird netting across the North Coast, ostensibly for the Common Quail, but the nets do not discriminate and each year millions of birds die on passage.

The Red Sea coast is very different. It runs some 800km from the Sudanese border north to Hurghada, where it splits into the western Gulf of Suez and the eastern Gulf of Aqaba. The Red Sea supports some of the richest (in terms of biodiversity) coral reefs in the world, as well as extensive mangroves. Bird species include breeding populations of the near-endemic White-eyed Gull and Sooty Gull, terns such as Caspian, White-cheeked, Lesser Crested, Crested and Bridled, Brown Boobies, and one of the densest breeding populations of Ospreys.

Mainland Egypt consists mostly of desert, split between the **Western Desert** west of the Nile and the **Eastern Desert** to the east. The former is a vast expanse of relatively low-lying, flat *hamada* desert – indeed the Qattara Depression to the north lies up to 134m below sea level. Running diagonally across the Western Desert from northwest to southeast is an extensive area of dune-land known as the Great Sand Sea, while in the southwestern corner are some of the driest and hottest places on the planet, but even here life persists. Characteristic species include Desert and Bar-tailed Larks, and the White-crowned Wheatear. Scattered across the Western Desert are a series of oases – Kharga, Dakhla, Farafra, Bahariya, and to the west Siwa – referred to here collectively as the **Western Oases**. These outposts, plus many much smaller and isolated oases, including acacia groves in the Qattara Depression, not only support populations of breeding species but during spring and autumn attract legions of migrating birds. At these times of year any pocket of vegetation in the vastness of the desert is worth checking out for migrants. Whereas in the Nile Valley the Hooded Crow is the common crow species, over much of the Western Desert and indeed Eastern Desert, the all-black Brown-necked Raven is prevalent.

To the east, the **Eastern Desert** is very different. This is mountainous desert that runs north from the border with Sudan to Suez and is riddled east and west with deep wadis, of which Wadi Degla, just outside Cairo, is one of the most northerly. While some species are shared with its western counterpart, distinctive birds of the Eastern Desert include breeding Egyptian Vultures, and Lappet-faced Vultures, Scrub Warblers, and Trumpeter Finches (also found in the Western Oases). In the very southeasternmost corner of Egypt's Eastern Desert, in the Halaib Triangle mentioned above, a number of species found nowhere else in Egypt breed on and around Gebel Elba, such as the Shining Sunbird and Fulvous Babbler.

Separating the Western and Eastern Deserts is the Nile Valley, referred to here simply as the **Valley**, which runs its way north via a large curve at modern Qena to the great fan of the Nile Delta, referred to here as the **Delta**. This is a landscape almost entirely moulded by humans, having been settled for much of the last 5,000 years. Very few areas of natural Nilotic vegetation remain, most notably on Ghazal and Saluga Islands just to the south of Aswan, and to the north of the High Dam. South of the High Dam the Valley has been flooded by the artificial creation of Lake Nasser. Today this lake not only supports Egypt's last population of Nile Crocodiles but also large populations of wintering waterfowl, waders and the bulk of Egypt's breeding population of the Egyptian Goose. In recent decades the African Pied Wagtail has established itself as a breeding resident on the lake shores, while other African species, such as the Pink-backed Pelican, Yellow-billed Stork, and Namaqua Dove, are now regular visitors.

North of Aswan, the Valley and Delta support an avifauna in some ways familiar to a visitor with European experience but in other ways distinctive. The House Sparrow is one of the most common species in and around Cairo, but then so is the Common Bulbul, and while the Eurasian Collared Dove has established a foothold in Egypt, the common urban dove is the Laughing Dove. Even in central Cairo a walk along the Nile can reveal the Little Bittern, Cattle Egret, Squacco Heron, and Little and Great Egrets.

A number of African species make their way down the Nile to Egypt. One of the characteristic birds of the river is the Pied Kingfisher, which is readily seen hovering just as depicted by the ancient Egyptians. Another kingfisher, the White-throated Kingfisher, is a recent colonist that has rapidly expanded its range west to Faiyum, and south at least as far as Minya, with unconfirmed reports from Luxor. Other African species include the Senegal Thick-knee, Kittlitz's Plover, and Senegal Coucal. In the countryside the Black-winged Kite, Little Green Bee-eater, and Crested Lark are familiar species, while the Delta is a stronghold for the secretive Painted Snipe.

Egypt is contiguous with the Middle East, or was until the completion of the Suez Canal in 1869, through the Sinai Peninsula, an inverted triangle of land some 61,000km² in area. While the north is relatively low lying, with sandy plains and low hills, a dominant feature of the south is the mountainous area around Saint Catherine, famous for its monastery and Mount Sinai (though at 2,641m Gebel Katrin is the highest point). Characteristic birds of these mountains include the Chukar, White-spectacled Bulbul, Palestine Sunbird, Tristram's Starling, and Sinai Rosefinch. While Hume's Owl is also found very sparsely in the Eastern Desert and Arabia, southern Sinai at Wadi Feiran probably affords the best chance of finding this rare and little-known species. In the northeasternmost corner of Sinai a number of species, such as the Syrian Woodpecker, Great Tit, and Serin, more widespread elsewhere in the Region, just creep into Egypt in and around Rafah.

Sinai thus provides a neat bridge into the region widely known as the Middle East. Covering the modern states detailed above, the Region is widely stereotyped, just as Egypt is, as a desert region. While this may be a true picture at least in part – the vast Arabian Desert, for example, dominates that peninsula – just as in Egypt, the desert regions are surprisingly varied. The landscape in north Syria is dominated in the east by the Syrian Desert, which is largely flat and low lying, while to the west it becomes more mountainous, culminating in Syria's highest peak, Mt Hermon at 2,814m. To the south, and sharing a Mediterranean coast, lies Lebanon, dominated by the Lebanon Mountains, rising to more than 3,000m. A major feature is the Bekaa Valley, running parallel to the coast and the source of the Asi and Litani Rivers. At one time these mountains were heavily forested with various *Pinus* species, oaks, and of course the Lebanese Cedar. Today little of these forests remains, almost entirely due to human agency. Much of western Syria, Lebanon, parts of western Jordan and the coastal areas to the south are termed collectively here as the **Levant** for brevity rather than historical accuracy. This area includes a number of very localized species, including those rare elsewhere in the region, such as the Black Francolin, breeding Lesser Kestrel, Eurasian Scops Owl, and enigmatic Syrian Serin. In southern Syria and northern Jordan, an unusually dark form of the Desert Lark is found.

Moving south towards the Arabian Peninsula, the area is dominated by the Naqab Desert and the desert tracts of Jordan from the Dead Sea east towards Iraq. Again for convenience rather than geographic accuracy, these areas are collectively referred to as the **Naqab**. One of the most spectacular and most visited sites in Jordan is the Nabataean city of Petra. Here, watch out for Fan-tailed Ravens, Tristram's Starlings, and Sinai Rosefinches. The shores of the Dead Sea, the lowest-lying place on the planet, are home to the diminutive and local near-endemic Dead Sea Sparrow.

The Arabian Peninsula, referred to in the text as **Arabia**, is the world's largest peninsula at some 3,237,500km^2, the vast majority of which is the state of Saudi Arabia. It has no permanent rivers and has a predominantly hot and very dry climate, with local exceptions discussed below.

The western coastline of the Arabian Peninsula borders the Red Sea and shares much of the avifauna of the Egyptian Red Sea. However, in the southeast there are breeding colonies of Pink-backed Pelicans, Saunder's Little Terns (recently confirmed in Egypt), and Brown Noddys. The taxonomic status of the Mangrove Reed Warbler, which breeds in the southern mangroves, is under debate. The western part of Arabia is defined by the Hijaz and Asir Mountains that run parallel to the coast from north of Taif south to the highlands of Yemen. This southeastern corner of the Arabian Peninsula is fascinating from an ornithological perspective, with a variety of species endemic to the peninsula, such as the Arabian Woodpecker, Yemen Warbler, Yemen Thrush, Arabian Waxbill, and Arabian and Yemen Serins. A number of African species are also found here, such as the Hamerkop and Little Rock Thrush.

Perhaps the most interesting area of the southern part of the Arabian Peninsula is the southern Oman region of Dhofar. The climate here is governed by the summer monsoon, supporting a very different flora and fauna to most of the peninsula. While much of northern Oman supports species from the Western Palearctic and Oriental biomes, Dhofar has many Afrotropical species, such as Bruce's Green Pigeon, African Paradise Flycatcher, Abyssinian White-eye, and Rüppell's Weaver. Macqueen's Bustard also breeds here. On the coast of the Gulf of Aden and Arabian Sea, the Brown Booby is joined by breeding colonies of the Masked Booby, while offshore look out for seabird species such as the Persian Shearwater, which also breeds, and Jouanin's Petrel.

Much of Oman's interior and the north include a more desert avifauna that has a closer affinity to the Western Palearctic and Oriental faunal regions. In the mountains that rise from the shores of the Gulf of Oman, Hume's Wheatear is a distinctive species, while the familiar Chukar is largely replaced by Arabian and Sand Partridges. In Muscat at Al Qurm Park, the Grey Francolin occurs alongside the Red-wattled Lapwing, Indian Roller, and Purple Sunbird.

The countries of the eastern Arabian Peninsula, namely the United Arab Emirates (UAE), Qatar, Bahrain, and Kuwait, are for the most part very hot throughout the year, with very little rainfall. Here, these countries and the coastal regions of Saudi Arabia along the Arabian Gulf are collectively termed the **Gulf**. Many of the birds here are desert species such as the Black-crowned Sparrow-lark, Greater Hoopoe Lark, Temminck's Lark, and in summer the Rufous-tailed Scrub Robin. In winter Kuwait offers a good chance of seeing the Grey Hypocolius, a regional specialty. The gardens of the UAE and neighboring states are also good for native White-eared and White-spectacled Bulbuls, and introduced Red-whiskered and Red-vented Bulbuls.

The Arabian Gulf also supports important breeding colonies of seabirds, including the near-endemic Socotra Cormorant. Other species include terns such as White-cheeked and Bridled Terns, and the Sooty Gull. The enigmatic Crab Plover breeds here in colonies, the only wader to nest in self-excavated burrows. Its range extends around the Arabian coast and it also breeds on the shores of the Arabian Red Sea, dispersing in winter. The mangroves support many heron and egret species and, just as in the Red Sea, breeding Western Reef Herons and Eurasian Spoonbills.

Migration

Bird migration is one of the great enigmas and spectacles of the natural world, and Egypt and the Middle East constitute a region at the very hub of one of the great migration corridors of the world. Many smaller species, including the vast majority of passerines, migrate on a broad front, but the larger birds – the large raptors, cranes, pelicans, storks, and others – are channeled through specific corridors. These species rely on thermals of hot air to provide them with lift and drive as they travel vast distances between northern breeding grounds and southern wintering grounds either within the Region or farther south, often in sub-Saharan Africa. That these corridors are predictable and geographically specific makes the Region one of the most sought-after locations for birdwatchers.

Having bred in Europe and western Asia, many of the larger species head south in autumn, after exploiting fully the rich food resources of their summer breeding quarters. Open flight across the Mediterranean or any other area of open sea is too energy sapping and inefficient for these birds, which rely on rising columns of hot air known as thermals to maintain their height and distance. The Bosphorus in northwestern Turkey is a major migration hub, as the birds head south through Syria and Lebanon and continue down the Mediterranean coast, and also through the northern extremities of the Great Rift Valley down to Sinai. Northern Sinai in autumn is a fabulous location to witness this fly-past, but the birds continue south on both sides of the Red Sea. In Egypt, Suez at the head of the Gulf of Aqaba and Ras Mohamed at the southern tip of Sinai can host thousands upon thousands of migrating raptors and other large birds. North of the tourist resorts of Hurghada and the Red Sea, Gebel Zeit at the mouth of the Gulf of Suez is an amazing migration hub. The Nile Valley is also a major corridor.

In spring the corridor reverses – not exactly but broadly – and the birds make their way north back to their breeding grounds. April at Ain Suhkna south of Suez is a prime migration hotspot. Here the high cliffs that tower over the small town, now a major resort, provide thermals and hence impetus to the vast flocks as they head north. There are few greater spectacles in the natural world.

It is not just the big birds, though. Egypt and the Middle East lie between the breeding and wintering grounds of many hundreds of other migratory birds, from swallows, martins, pipits and wagtails, warblers, and flycatchers, to chats, finches, and buntings. Some stay over winter, while others head still farther south even as far as South Africa. In spring and autumn, when this great movement takes place, virtually any garden, tussock, farm or oasis is worth a stop, and scanning any area of water, however ephemeral, is worthwhile for waders, waterfowl, crakes or even marsh terns such as the Whiskered Tern or the stunning White-winged Tern, although the latter also breeds along the Gulf. In Cairo one of the joys of spring occurs from mid-April onwards, when huge flocks of migrating European Bee-eaters pass over, heading north. The Blue-cheeked Bee-eater also passes through, although some individuals remain to breed.

Elsewhere in the Region the pattern remains the same, with any area of water or vegetation, however small or remote, worth inspecting. Bird migration does not recognize national boundaries or distance. In summer 2020 a paper delivered at the annual conference of the Ornithological Society of the Middle East (OSME) reported that a Common Cuckoo that had been ringed in Mongolia, had headed south and west over Asia, across Arabia to Socotra (politically part of Yemen), and on to East Africa. That this was also part of an educational project between schools in Mongolia and Yemen (Socotra) truly reflects the international nature of bird migration.

How To Use This Book

Each of the 280 bird species most likely to be encountered in Egypt and the Region has its own entry accompanied by a photograph showing the bird in typical plumage. Where there are major differences between the sexes or over seasons, subsidiary photographs are included. Where similar species have been identified in the text, a thumbnail showing these birds is included where space permits. The species order follows that of the latest official EORC Checklist of 2019. Where the species has never been recorded in Egypt but is found elsewhere in the Region, the order generally follows that published by the OSME. The species descriptions are organized as follows.

SPECIES NAME & MEASUREMENTS

Both the common English name and scientific name are provided. The English name in **bold** is the most widely accepted name across the literature and generally follows the name used in the official EORC Checklist of Egyptian Birds. However, names are constantly changing. Where there are widely used alternative names, these are given in parentheses below the main names. The scientific name in *italics* again generally follows the EORC Checklist. Taxonomy is constantly changing and occasionally there are differences associated with such changes. For instance, the Great Grey Shrike *Lanius excubitor* in the current book follows the latest edition of Svennson, Mullarney, & Zetterstrom, but in the Checklist appears as the Southern Grey Shrike *L.meridionalis*. Other examples include Barbary Falcon *Falco pelegrinoides* and Pharaoh Eagle Owl *Bubo ascalaphus*. These taxonomic discrepancies may have little impact on the ID for the average observer in the field.

The length of each bird is given in centimetres. Where there is a substantial difference in length between races or sexes, a range may be given. For instance, in many raptors the female is often larger than the male. In birds such as bee-eaters and terns, where there are long tail streamers adding greatly to the length, these are further detailed in parentheses with an approximate length in centimetres. For larger species or for species most often seen in flight, the wingspan (abbreviated to WS) is also included.

DESCRIPTION

A short general description is given for each species, followed by overall plumage details and bare parts (bill, legs, and so on) using the descriptors in the glossary. Differences between the sexes or seasonal plumages, and distinctive juvenile plumage, are described if important, as well as details of the bird's appearance in flight. Similar species, named in **bold**, perhaps less common or less likely to be seen, may also be briefly described after the description of the main species.

VOICE

Transcribing bird song and calls into the written word can be very challenging. The renderings generally follow the key literature on the birds of the region, augmented by the author's own field experience. Many migratory species with distinctive songs on their extralimital breeding grounds do not normally sing on passage, such as the Common Nightingale and many warblers, so no detailed rendering of their full song is given. However, many species have distinctive contact or alarm calls and these are described.

DISTRIBUTION

For each species, the distribution is given within Egypt using the geographical areas described in the section on the biogeography of Egypt and the Middle East. A brief assessment of its status is also given. The distribution and status within the Region is then provided, again using the geographical areas described earlier.

Resident Species present throughout the year and breeds.
Summer breeder Species breeds, but only as a summer visitor.
Winter Species does not breed and occurs only during the winter.
Passage Species occurs on migration in spring and autumn.

The above are not mutually exclusive – a species may occur on migration, but some individuals may also stay and overwinter. Some species are very local while others may be more widespread, and on migration a species may be seen almost anywhere.

HABITAT & HABITS

The key habitats in which a species is likely to be encountered are then detailed, although note the above point about migratory species. Where space permits, key behavioural details may be highlighted, or any distinctive traits such as tail fanning, wagging or cocking, distinctive flight patterns, associated species or anything else that may aid identification

GLOSSARY

aberrant Abnormal or unusual.
Acacia Important genus of desert/semi-desert/savannah trees, e.g. acacia groves.
adult Mature; capable of breeding.
aerial Making use of the open sky.
aquatic Living on or in water.
arboreal Living in trees.
canopy Leafy foliage of tree-tops.
cheek Term loosely applied to sides of head, below eye or on ear-coverts.
collar Distinctive band of color that encircles or partly encircles neck.
coverts Small feathers on wings (lesser, median, greater, primary, and so on), ear and tail-base.
crepuscular Active at dusk and dawn.
crest Extended feathers on head.

crown Top of head.

crown-stripe Distinct line from forehead along centre of crown.

culmen Top edge of upper mandible.

ear-coverts Feathers covering ear opening. Often distinctly colored.

eclipse Non-breeding plumage of ducks where males often look much like females.

endemic Indigenous and confined to particular place or region.

eye-ring Contrasting ring around eye.

eye-stripe Stripe through eye.

extinct No longer in existence.

family Specified group of genera.

foraging Search for food.

flank Side of body.

foreneck Lower throat.

form Broadly synonymous with subspecies.

gape Basal part of beak.

genus Group of related species.

hackles Long and pointed neck feathers.

hepatic Refers to rust- or liver-colored plumage phase, mainly in female cuckoos.

immature Not yet adult.

iris Colored eye membrane surrounding pupil.

juvenile Young – in first plumage of bird.

khorr Flooded or seasonally flooded desert valley, for example on Lake Nasser.

lanceolate Lance shaped; slim and pointed.

lore(s) Between base of bill and eye.

malar Stripe on side of throat.

mandible Each of two parts of bill.

mangroves Trees of various species, such as *Avicennia* spp., forming important intertidal habitat.

mantle Back, between wings.

mask Dark plumage around eyes and ear-coverts.

morph One of several distinct types of plumage in the same species.

moult Seasonal shedding of plumage.

nape Back of neck.

nocturnal Active at night.

nominate First subspecies to be formally named.

non-passerine All orders of birds except passerines.

oasis More or less isolated water source and vegetation in desert.

order Group of related families.

Palearctic Old World and arctic zone.

passerine Member of the order Passeriformes, commonly known as perching birds.

pelagic Ocean-going.

pied Black and white.

plumage Feathers of a bird.

primaries Outer flight feathers in wing.

primary projection On resting bird, projection of primaries beyond tertials.

race Subspecies.

range Geographical area or areas inhabited by a species.

raptors Birds of prey and vultures, excluding owls.

rump Lower back.

scapulars Feathers along edge of mantle.

scree Loose boulders, rocks, and stones at bases or lower slopes of cliffs – also talus.

speculum Area of color on secondary feathers of wings, for example in ducks.

spangles Distinctive white or shimmering spots in plumage.

species Groups of birds reproductively isolated from other such groups.

streamers Long extensions to feathers, usually of tail.

subspecies Distinct form that does not have specific status.

supercilium Streak above eye.

talons Strong, sharp claws used to seize or kill prey.

tarsus Lower part of leg.

terminal band Broad band on tip of feather or tail.

tertials Innermost wing-coverts, often covering secondaries.

trousers Feathered legs of large birds of prey, for example *Aquila* eagles.

underparts Undersurface of bird from throat to vent.

underwing Undersurface of wing including linings and flight feathers.

underwing-coverts Plumage covering underside bases of primaries and secondaries.

undertail-coverts Plumage covering tail-base beyond vent.

upperparts Upper surface of bird, including wings, back, and tail.

uppertail-coverts Plumage covering base of uppertail below rump.

upperwing-coverts Plumage covering upperside bases of primaries and secondaries.

vagrant Accidental, irregular.

vent Undertail area.

wadi Seasonal or dry desert valley.

wing-coverts Small feathers on wing at bases of primaries and secondaries.

wingspan Length from one wing-tip to the other when fully extended.

winter plumage Plumage seen during non-breeding winter months.

Egyptian Goose ■ *Alopochen aegyptiaca* 70cm WS 144cm

DESCRIPTION Distinctive small goose. Brown-buff above; darker on back and rump with pale grey underparts and buff on breast with dark spot. Neck and head pale grey with dark brown patch around eye and dark collar. Tail black. Bill pink with black tip. Legs dark red and rather long. In flight note white wing-panels and green speculum. **VOICE** Braying *haah haah haah…* and hissing. **DISTRIBUTION** In Egypt common resident in Nile Valley from Aswan south, sometimes in large flocks with winter dispersal north to Cairo. Feral population in UAE and escapes recorded elsewhere. **HABITAT AND HABITS** Large inland waters including lakes and rivers. Grazes on fields and grassland.

Ruddy Shelduck ■ *Tadorna ferruginea* 64cm WS 130cm

DESCRIPTION Size of small goose. Adult bright cinnamon-brown throughout with black tail. Head and neck pale buff with narrow black collar (absent in female and non-breeding male). Bill black. Legs black. In flight shows black flight feathers, bold white panel, and dark green speculum. **Common Shelduck** *T. tadorna*, black and white with bottle-green head, chestnut breast-band, and red bill, is passage and winter visitor. **VOICE** Nasal honking and strident *aang* in flight. **DISTRIBUTION** In Egypt rare in winter and on passage to Delta and Valley; also north Sinai. In Region in winter and on passage especially in Levant. May breed in eastern Arabia. **HABITAT AND HABITS** Generally inland on lake shores, along riversides and marshes, wet fields, and pasture.

Ruddy Shelduck

Common Shelduck

Eurasian Wigeon ■ *Anas penelope* 48cm WS 80cm

DESCRIPTION Rather small, rounded duck. Male largely grey above and on flanks. Breast pinkish-brown and belly white. Head rounded; chestnut-brown with forehead to crown pale buff. Bill small, pale grey, and with black tip. Female darkish grey-brown; more reddish below with white belly. Bill as male. In flight pointed tail and in male large white patch on wing. **VOICE** Male has loud, whistled *weeeooo* and female a growl. **DISTRIBUTION** Throughout Egypt and Region widespread winter visitor and on passage. **HABITAT AND HABITS** Areas of fresh water such as marshes, lakes, and rivers. On passage also on coastal lagoons, estuaries, and salt marshes.

Gadwall ■ *Anas strepera* 52cm WS 88cm

DESCRIPTION Slightly smaller than Mallard (p. 16). Male appears rather uniform grey at any distance, but with clear black rear. At closer range note brownish-grey head and small white patch on wing with chestnut and black in flight. Bill dark. Female similar to female Mallard but with greyer head, pale throat, and dark bill with orange sides. In flight note white belly and white speculum. **VOICE** Short *arkh*, Mallard-like quacking. **DISTRIBUTION** In Egypt in small numbers in winter in Delta and Valley and northern lakes. Occasional elsewhere. In Region widespread throughout in winter and on passage. **HABITAT AND HABITS** Wetland areas including lakes, rivers, and marshes, but rarely on coast.

Eurasian Teal ■ *Anas crecca* L 36cm WS 61cm

DESCRIPTION Smallest dabbling duck. Male small, compact duck, largely grey with white stripe sometimes clear along side and black-bordered, buff rear. Head dark chestnut with glossy dark green around and behind eye edged with yellow. Breast buff, speckled

dark. Female like very small Mallard (below) – bill often with orange at base. Garganey (opposite) has plainer head pattern, smaller bill, and pale margin to tail. In flight shows glossy green speculum clearly bordered white. **VOICE** Male's clear whistle similar to Northern Pintail's (opposite); otherwise short, rather high-pitched quack. **DISTRIBUTION** Common throughout Egypt and Region, widespread winter visitor and on passage. **HABITAT AND HABITS** Areas of fresh water such as lakes and rivers. On passage also seen on coastal lagoons and estuaries.

Mallard ■ *Anas platyrhynchos* 55cm WS 93cm

DESCRIPTION Wild ancestor of domestic duck, to which other species can be compared. Male dark grey above; paler grey below with purple-brown breast and clear-cut black rear. Head bottle-green with thin white collar. Tail white. Bill yellow. Female mottled brown throughout with darker crown and eye-stripe. Bill dark orange. In flight shows bright blue speculum bordered white. **VOICE** Soft quack, harsher when agitated. **DISTRIBUTION** In Egypt widespread winter visitor and passage to Delta and Valley, Western Oases, and north Sinai. Local resident breeder, for example in Cairo. In Region, Levant, and scattered feral breeding populations in Arabia and Gulf. Widespread in winter throughout. **HABITAT AND HABITS** Any area of wetlands including lakes, rivers, and estuaries. Feral Mallards often have large patches of white.

Northern Pintail ▪ *Anas acuta* 56cm (excluding tail feathers of male) WS 85cm

DESCRIPTION Slim, elegant, long-necked duck. Male greyish above with white breast and underparts, and black rear. Head and neck chocolate-brown with white from behind eye down side of neck. Long, slender, pointed tail diagnostic. Bill slender and dark grey. Female as Mallard (opposite), but paler and slimmer with plain head and pointed tail. In flight shows dark green speculum (duller brown in female) with white trailing edge. **VOICE** Quacking as Mallard's. Male also has clear whistle. **DISTRIBUTION** Throughout Egypt and Region widespread winter visitor and on passage. **HABITATS AND HABITS** Large, shallow inland lakes and lagoons. In winter also brackish lakes and estuaries. In mixed species flocks note long neck, rather small head and pointed tail.

Garganey ▪ *Anas querquedula* 38cm WS 63cm

DESCRIPTION Only slightly larger than Eurasian Teal (opposite). Male has dark brown head, neck, and breast, with striking white crescent from above and in front of eye tapering around down nape-side. Flanks pale and finely barred. Bill dark. Female like small Mallard (opposite), but with head more strongly marked and white spot at bill-base. In flight male shows pale blue-grey on forewing; both sexes broad white trailing edge. **VOICE** Weak, rather high-pitched quacking. **DISTRIBUTION** In Egypt widespread passage migrant, especially in autumn along North Coast. In Region widespread throughout on passage. A few winter. Has bred in Levant. **HABITAT AND HABITS** Areas of fresh water such as lakes and rivers. On passage seen on coastal lagoons and estuaries, for example in north Sinai.

Northern Shoveler ▪ *Anas clypeata* 50cm WS 78cm

DESCRIPTION Distinctive, huge-billed duck. Male largely black and white above; white below with black rear and chestnut belly and flanks. Head glossy, bottle-green. Iris yellow. Bill very long, heavy, and spatulate. Female as female Mallard (p. 16), but with darker belly and huge bill. In flight green/dull green speculum with no white trailing edge. Male with pale blue forewing. **VOICE** Male utters sharp *tuk tuk* when flushed. Also quacking. **DISTRIBUTION** Throughout Egypt and Region widespread winter visitor and on passage. Very local breeder in Syria. **HABITAT AND HABITS** Areas of fresh water such as lakes and rivers. On passage also coastal lagoons and estuaries.

Common Pochard ▪ *Aythya ferina* 47cm WS 77cm

DESCRIPTION Distinctive profile with concave bill along sloping forehead to peaked crown. Male grey above, and on flanks and belly. Breast, rear, and tail black. Head and neck chestnut. Iris red. Bill dark with pale grey band. Female has brown breast and grey-buff head and neck. In flight wings grey-brown with no speculum. Scarce **Red-crested Pochard** *Netta rufina* male has similar pattern but darker on back, glowing dark orange on head,

and scarlet bill. Female has pale cheeks. **VOICE** Quiet, but male may utter low whistle and female harsher *kraa kraa*. **DISTRIBUTION** Throughout Egypt and Region widespread winter visitor and on passage. **HABITAT AND HABITS** Areas of fresh water including marshes, lakes, and rivers. On passage also coastal lagoons, estuaries, and salt marshes.

Ferruginous Duck ■ *Aythya nyroca* 40cm WS 65cm

DESCRIPTION Smaller than Common Pochard (opposite). Male deep chestnut throughout; very dark on back. Bright white rear end sharply demarcated. Head has steep forehead and peaked crown. Iris white. Bill blue-grey with black tip. In flight note white belly and large white wing-patches. Female similarly dark but slightly less chestnut and with dark iris. Head profile and, in flight, more white on wing separates species from female Tufted Duck (below). **VOICE** Quiet; occasional *krr-err* in flight.
DISTRIBUTION In Egypt uncommon in winter in Delta and Valley south to Lake Nasser. In Region very local and scattered breeder in Levant and northern Arabia. Widespread but uncommon in winter and on passage. **HABITAT AND HABITS** Shallow freshwater lakes and marshes. Occasional saltwater on passage.

Tufted Duck ■ *Aythya fuligula* 44cm WS 68cm

DESCRIPTION Small, stocky duck. Male glossy black throughout, with white flanks, breast, and belly. Head has long, floppy crest from hindcrown. Female dark brown above with paler brown flanks, whitish belly, and short crest or 'tuft' (absent in Ferruginous Duck, above). Both sexes have yellow iris, and pale blue-grey bill with black tip. In flight note large white wing-bar. **VOICE** Growling *krr krr…* in female. **DISTRIBUTION** Common winter and passage visitor to Egypt, mostly in Delta and northern lakes through to north Sinai and south to Aswan. In Region widespread throughout in winter and on passage. **HABITAT AND HABITS** Lakes, reservoirs, rivers, and ponds, even in parks. In winter also along coasts. Often in flocks where black and white male distinctive.

Chukar ■ *Alectoris chukar* 34cm
(Chukar Partridge)

DESCRIPTION Boldly patterned partridge. Grey-blue tinged brown above, with grey-blue breast. Cream bib bordered with black, continuing through eye to lores and across

forehead. Obscure pale supercilium. Underparts fawn with dark and white striping. Grey rump with chestnut corners to tail. Bill, orbital ring, and legs red. **VOICE** Series of *chaks* building up and accelerating. **DISTRIBUTION** In Egypt common resident in mountains of northeast to south Sinai. In Region resident in Levant south through Naqab. Oman. Introduced in UAE. Similar **Barbary Partridge** *A. barbara* probably now extinct on Egypt's North Coast. **HABITAT AND HABITS** In Sinai in mountains. Elsewhere hillsides and rocky slopes to sea level in scrub, semi-deserts, and farmland. In small flocks on the ground; flies only when pressed.

Sand Partridge ■ *Ammoperdix heyi* 25cm

DESCRIPTION Small, rather uniform partridge. Male uniform pinkish-brown above with darker, greyer head and neck. Arabian race *intermedia* darker. Flanks have wavy stripes

of dark, rosy, and pale. Pale lores and white cheek-patch. Yellow bill. Pale legs. Female similar, but duller and paler and lacking white facial markings. In flight note chestnut corners to tail. **VOICE** Repeated *kwia kwia kwia* and sharper alarm call. **DISTRIBUTION** In Egypt common resident in Eastern Desert and south Sinai. In Region resident from Naqab south through much of Arabia and southern Gulf. **HABITAT AND HABITS** Deserts and semi-deserts, rocky hillsides, ravines, and wadi floors. Ground-living, generally foraging in small flocks, with larger numbers at water sources.

Grey Francolin ▪ *Francolinus pondicerianus* 30cm

DESCRIPTION Rather uniform, short-tailed, grey-brown game-bird. At close range finely mottled in greys, browns, and cream, with barred underparts. Chestnut forehead and cheeks and in male pale buff throat indistinctly bordered with black. Bill dark grey. Legs reddish with spurs in male. **Black Francolin** *F. francolinus*, local resident in Levant and introduced in UAE, has male black with white spots and chestnut collar, and female similar to Grey but with chestnut nape. **VOICE** Loud, penetrating *kik-kwye-ku, kik-kwye-ku, kik-kwye-ku*. **DISTRIBUTION** Not in Egypt. Introduced successfully into Gulf south to Oman. Range increasing. **HABITAT AND HABITS** Open thorn scrub and grassland, but increasingly in more urban environments (like Muscat), parks, roadsides, and cultivation. Not shy, often feeding in open.

Grey Francolin

Black Francolin

Quail ▪ *Coturnix coturnix* 17cm

DESCRIPTION Very small, rotund game-bird. Buff brown above, cryptically mottled dark brown and streaked cream. Cream belly and undertail-coverts. Complex head pattern with cream supercilium, dark through eye, and dark malar stripe. Male has variable dark throat; female has pale throat. **VOICE** Loud call, *pil pil-it*, often rendered 'wet-my-lips'. **DISTRIBUTION** In Egypt widespread on passage, especially along North Coast and Sinai. Some overwinter and local breeder. In Region localized summer breeder in Levant and parts of northern Arabia. Widespread elsewhere on passage. **HABITAT AND HABITS** Grassland, pastures, and meadows. On passage any area with grass scrub and thickets. Shy and very unobtrusive. Best located by sound. Most often seen when flushed, when note long, pointed wings and low flight, quickly making cover.

Little Grebe ▪ *Tachybaptus ruficollis* 27cm WS 43cm

DESCRIPTION Region's smallest grebe. Short-necked and dumpy with rounded rear. In summer very dark with paler rear. Head, neck, and breast blackish with deep maroon-red cheeks and throat. Bright yellow gape highly visible. Bill short and straight. In winter brownish-buff with dark back and crown and pale spot at bill-base. **VOICE**

High-pitched trill when breeding. **DISTRIBUTION** Common resident in Egypt, breeding in Delta and Western Oases. More widespread in winter, including in Sinai and Valley. Resident breeder and in winter in Levant. Localized breeder in Arabia and Gulf; more widespread in winter. **HABITAT AND HABITS** Freshwater lakes, ponds, and rivers. In winter and on passage also coastal wetlands. On water, size and dumpy, small-billed profile distinguish it from ducks. Dives when disturbed.

Great Crested Grebe ▪ *Podiceps cristatus* 50cm WS 85cm

DESCRIPTION Large grebe. Adult breeding dark brown above, white below with buffish flanks. Head has double black crest on crown. Erectile cheek-plumes orange bordered darker. Bill long and pointed. In

winter loses crest and plumes, white head with angular black crown, black lores, and pinkish bill. In flight prominent white 'shoulders'. **VOICE** Loud, nasal calls. Also shorter *krro*. **DISTRIBUTION** In Egypt former breeder in Delta. In winter and on passage fairly common through Valley and Western Oases. In Region, local resident breeder in Levant and eastern Arabia. In winter and on passage also to northern Red Sea and northern Gulf. **HABITAT AND HABITS** Freshwater lakes, ponds, and rivers. In winter and on passage also on coasts.

Black-necked Grebe ■ *Podiceps nigricollis* 31cm WS 58cm

DESCRIPTION Small, blunt-ended grebe. Breeding adult blackish above with chestnut flanks. Head and neck black with steep crown and yellow fan of feathers from behind eye.

Iris scarlet. Bill short, sharp, and up-tilted. In winter grey and black with white throat and front of neck with dark collar. **VOICE** Mournful whistle when breeding. **DISTRIBUTION** In Egypt common in winter and on passage in Delta and Valley, including northern lakes and Western Oases. In Region on passage and in winter throughout, with breeding populations in southern Gulf, Oman, and western Arabia. **HABITAT AND HABITS** Freshwater lakes, ponds, and rivers. In winter and on passage also coasts and estuaries. Dives. Red iris and bill profile distinguish it from Little Grebe (opposite) even at distance.

Cory's Shearwater ■ *Calonectris diomedea* 52cm WS 120cm

DESCRIPTION Large, heavy-billed shearwater. Upperparts, including head, grey-brown with mottling on back and mantle, and dark wings and tail. Underparts white with smudgy grey-brown on breast. Bill yellowish with dark near tip. In flight note white underside to wings with narrow brown margins. Could be mistaken for a gull, but flies on long, slender wings held bowed, gliding close to the water. East Mediterranean race *C. d. diomedea* sometimes separated as **Scopoli's Shearwater**. **VOICE** Silent away from breeding colonies. **DISTRIBUTION** In Egypt scarce on passage off Mediterranean coast, including Sinai and northern Red Sea. In Region on passage off Levant Mediterranean coast. **HABITAT AND HABITS** Pelagic but can be seen from shore. In winter mostly extralimital, but some remain in central Mediterranean.

Yelkouan Shearwater ■ *Puffinus yelkouan* 33cm WS 82cm

DESCRIPTION Medium-sized shearwater. Blackish-brown (appearing black at distance) above, including uppersides of wings and tail. Underparts pale below variably smudged brown, and with 'messy' border with dark upperparts. In flight note undersides of wings pale, smudged brown and bordered with dark brown. Feet project beyond tail. Off southern Arabia and Oman very similar **Persian Shearwater** *P. persicus* cleaner white below with suggestion of white forehead. **VOICE** Silent away from breeding colonies.

Yelkouan Shearwater   *Persian Shearwater*

DISTRIBUTION In Egypt throughout the year off Mediterranean coast. In Region off Levant Mediterranean coast, probably breeding in Aegean. **HABITAT AND HABITS** Pelagic. Flies low over the water, sometimes in large flocks, with stiff wings and rapid wingbeats interspersed with long glides.

Red-billed Tropicbird

■ *Phaethon aethereus* 100cm (including 50cm tail streamers) WS 105cm

DESCRIPTION Elegant white seabird with very long tail streamers. Adult white throughout with subtle dark barring on back and black wing-tips. Head all white with black eye-stripe. Bill bright red. Tail white, with very long central streamers. Immature has more barring, yellow bill with black tip, and no tail streamers. **VOICE** Rasping, shrill cries. **DISTRIBUTION** Local and uncommon breeder in Egyptian Red Sea. In Region resident breeder in southern Red Sea, south Arabia, and southern Gulf. Post-breeding dispersal throughout Red and Arabian Seas, and Gulf. **HABITAT AND HABITS**. Breeds on rocky sea cliffs, coasts, and offshore islands. Otherwise maritime. Highly aerial on long, pointed wings; active flight, often high, interspersed with glides and hovers before diving for fish. Will settle on the water.

Brown Booby ■ *Sula leucogaster* 70cm WS 145cm

DESCRIPTION Large, strictly marine relative of gannets. Adult deep chocolate-brown above, including head, throat, and chest. White below, sharply demarcated. Pale facial skin – blue around eye – and long, pale, yellowish/pinkish bill. Tail pointed and dark brown. **Masked Booby** S. *dactylatra* similar in form but all white with black facial mask, tail, and trailing edges to wings. **VOICE** Loud, grating honks at colonies. **DISTRIBUTION** In Egypt in Red Sea, breeding from Hurghada south with dispersal to Gulfs of Aqaba and Suez. In Region breeds along Red Sea and south Arabian coasts. Masked Booby breeds south Arabia only. **HABITAT AND HABITS** Breeds on rocky offshore islands. Otherwise coastal and maritime. Can be seen perching on buoys and similar. Plunge dives for fish.

Brown Booby   *Masked Booby*

Great Cormorant ■ *Phalacrocorax carbo* 85cm WS 140cm

DESCRIPTION Large, all-dark waterbird. Breeding adult oily black throughout glossed blue/green – bronzed on wing. White cheeks and chin, yellow chin-patch, and short, angular crest. In flight dark with white flank-patch. Adult winter and juvenile duller. Bill straight with hooked tip. Swims low with bill angled upwards. **VOICE** Guttural calls but generally silent in Region. **DISTRIBUTION** In Egypt common winter visitor and on passage to all coasts and to large inland lakes, including Nasser and Nile. In Region widespread throughout in winter and on passage. **HABITAT AND HABITS** Coasts, lagoons, and offshore islands. Lakes, brackish and fresh, and rivers. Can be seen in large flocks of many hundreds of birds, in flight flying in lines. Floats low in the water and dives for fish.

Socotra Cormorant ■
Phalacrocorax nigrogularis 80cm WS 130cm

DESCRIPTION Slightly smaller and much slimmer than Great Cormorant (p. 25). Breeding adult all black with white line behind eye (hard to see in the field). Slimmer head and neck than Great, with much more slender bill and in flight no white flank-spot. Adult winter duller. Juvenile browner, pale below. **VOICE** Largely silent except in breeding colonies. **DISTRIBUTION** Endemic breeder to the Gulf, southern Arabia, and Socotra. Dispersal in winter, including to southern Red Sea but not Egypt. **HABITAT AND HABITS** Nests in large colonies mainly on offshore islands; also cliffs. Otherwise largely coastal and at sea. Often found feeding in large flocks, swimming low in the water and diving for fish. In flight often in lines low over water.

White Pelican ■ *Pelecanus onocrotalus* 160cm WS 290cm
(Great White Pelican)

DESCRIPTION Enormous white waterbird tinged yellow-pink below, especially on breast. Floppy crest on nape and pale pink facial skin. Huge bill greyish with yellow pouch.

Juvenile much greyer and browner above than adult. Legs short and yellowish. In flight contrasting black flight feathers, neck retracted, and legs not projecting beyond tail. **VOICE** Quiet except in breeding colonies. **DISTRIBUTION** In Egypt on passage in Delta and Valley south to Lake Nasser. Rare in winter. Also north Sinai and Red Sea coast. In Region on passage throughout except south and east Arabia. **HABITAT AND HABITS** Wetlands including large lakes, reservoirs, rivers, and coastal lagoons. On migration in small to large flocks often flying in formation, when superficially like White Stork (p. 34), but neck retracted and bare parts not red.

Pink-backed Pelican

■ *Pelecanus rufescens* 130cm WS 275cm

DESCRIPTION Enormous off-white waterbird (but smaller than White Pelican, opposite). Greyish-white tinged pink above when breeding. Small, angular crest. Facial skin pale with black spot at bill-base. Bill horn colored with pale pouch. Juvenile duller and browner than adult. Legs yellowish. In flight as White but flight feathers duller, greyer, and less contrasting. **VOICE** Quiet except in breeding colonies. **DISTRIBUTION** In Egypt on passage only on Lake Nasser. Elsewhere in Region resident breeder only in southeast Arabia. Some dispersal east and north in winter. **HABITAT AND HABITS** Coastal lagoons, sandbanks, and mangroves. In Egypt lake shores on Lake Nasser, where a relatively recent colonist. Generally in singles or small flocks.

Little Bittern ■ *Ixobrychus minutus* 35cm WS 55cm

DESCRIPTION Smallest heron in area. Pigeon sized. Male black above and on crown, with contrasting whitish-buff on wings and underparts. Almost black and white in flight.

Female duller brown above and more streaked below. Juvenile more heavily streaked. Bill yellowish. Legs yellow-green. Flight slow and noticeably jerky; appears short tailed with legs projecting. **VOICE** Alarm call sharp *krak*. **DISTRIBUTION** In Egypt resident and summer breeder in Delta and northern Valley. More widespread on passage and in winter. In Region widespread on passage with very localized breeding in Arabia and Levant. **HABITAT AND HABITS** Wetlands, riversides (even in central Cairo), reedbeds, and irrigation canals. Secretive and female especially cryptic, clambering around in vegetation. Male very distinctive in flight. Breeds in loose colonies in reedbeds.

Black-crowned Night Heron ■ *Nycticorax nycticorax* 62cm WS 110cm

DESCRIPTION Thickset, heavy-billed heron. Adult pale grey to whitish below; darker on wings with black back and crown. Slender white plumes from behind eye. Bill dark, relatively short, and heavy. Iris red. Legs yellowish. In flight dumpy; light grey with black back. Juvenile distinct – largely brown with pale spots. **VOICE** Raucous at breeding

colonies. Main call croaking *quark*. **DISTRIBUTION** In Egypt probable resident breeder in southern Valley. More widespread and common in winter in Delta and Valley. Localized summer breeder in Levant and localized resident breeder in eastern Arabia. Widespread in winter/on passage. **HABITAT AND HABITS** Wetlands, rivers, lakes, and marshes. Unobtrusive by day; generally perched in trees and dense vegetation at waterside. Often in small flocks in flight, at dusk dispersing to feeding areas.

Juvenile

Striated Heron ■ *Butorides striata* 45cm WS 60cm
(Green-backed Heron)

DESCRIPTION Similar in size to Squacco Heron (opposite) but much darker. Adult dumpy. Largely dark blue-grey to brownish-grey; upperparts have pale feather fringes. Black crown and cheek-stripe. Grey neck. Juvenile streaked below. Bill long and largely yellowish.

Legs yellow. In flight stocky; plain dark above. **VOICE** When flushed croaky *kweeoo*. **DISTRIBUTION** In Egypt breeding resident along Red Sea coast and south Sinai. Also Nile Valley north to Cairo, with recent range expansion. Elsewhere all Arabian coasts except northern Gulf. **HABITAT AND HABITS** Coasts and offshore islands including mangroves. Along Nile, in areas of dense vegetation even in Cairo. At rest appears dark and thickset, but neck can be extended as it lunges for prey, creating a more slender impression.

Squacco Heron ▪ *Ardeola ralloides* 45cm WS 85cm

DESCRIPTION Small, squat heron. At rest adult often appears hunched. Largely buff-beige in summer with streaked nape-plumes. Non-breeding has streaked neck and breast. In flight transformed, appearing very white due to pure white wings. Bill dark with yellow base. Legs yellowish. **VOICE** Rather coarse *karr*. **DISTRIBUTION** In Egypt local breeder in southern Valley. Common in winter and on passage throughout Delta and Valley. Local from Western Oases to North Coast including Sinai. In Region common on passage throughout – some winter and localized breeder in Levant and Arabia. **HABITAT AND HABITS** Riversides, marshes, ponds, lakes, and ditches. Easily overlooked in dense vegetation and reeds or skulking along canal banks, until gleaming white of wings is revealed. Colonial breeder but otherwise mostly solitary.

Cattle Egret ▪ *Bubulcus ibis* 50cm WS 85cm
(Western Cattle Egret)

DESCRIPTION Small, thickset egret. All white but shorter necked than Little Egret (p. 31). In summer buff on crown and breast. In villages often discolored dirty grey. Bill short, usually yellow-grey, although dark in juvenile. Legs yellowish-grey. Stocky in flight. **VOICE** Colonies noisy. In flight soft croak. **DISTRIBUTION** In Egypt widespread and common in Delta and Valley, Western Oases, and across North Coast to Sinai. Breeds in localized colonies in Delta and Valley. In Region widespread in winter and on passage. Breeding in Levant, Gulf, and very locally Arabia. **HABITAT AND HABITS** Farmland, parks, and gardens; also towns and villages on refuse dumps and similar. Attends livestock in fields. Roosts in colonies in trees, and small flocks can be seen heading for roosts at dusk, often in 'V' formation.

Western Reef Heron ■ *Egretta gularis* 64cm WS 90cm

(Reef Heron, Western Reef Egret)

DESCRIPTION Coastal egret occurring in two color forms. White phase very similar to Little Egret (opposite), all white with greyish-black legs and dull yellowish lower legs and feet. Bill yellowish, sometimes with darker base. Lores pale. Dark phase blackish to dark grey in good light – with white throat. **VOICE** Guttural *kraak*. **DISTRIBUTION** In Egypt resident restricted to Red Sea coast and south Sinai, where breeds in colonies in mangroves and on offshore islands. Elsewhere in Region resident around entire Arabian coast except south. **HABITAT AND HABITS** Coastal, where needs to be checked against Little, but note bare parts. On mudflats and beaches, but also rocky coastline. Can be very confiding. Often stalks along tidal mark, dashing out and lunging at prey.

Light morph

Dark morph

Little Egret ▪ *Egretta garzetta* 60cm WS 90cm

DESCRIPTION Elegant all-white egret. Much smaller than Great Egret (below), slimmer, and thinner billed. White throughout, in summer with two slender white plumes from behind eye and lace-like plumes from back and belly. Bill long, slender, and black. Legs black with bright yellow feet. **VOICE** Generally silent. Call crow-like *aaagh*. More vocal at breeding colonies. **DISTRIBUTION** In Egypt widespread in winter and on passage. Localized breeding resident in Delta and Valley. In Region widespread on passage and in winter. Local breeder in Levant north to southern Syria. **HABITAT AND HABITS** Wetlands including lakes, rivers, irrigation canals, marshes, and brackish and coastal waters. Stalks in shallow water, chasing and lunging after prey, when yellow feet often very clear. Nests in colonies, often with other heron and egret species.

Great Egret ▪ *Egretta alba* 95cm WS 155cm
(Western Great Egret, Great White Egret, Great White Heron)

DESCRIPTION Largest egret in region. Larger than Grey Heron (p. 32) and white throughout. Long neck often extended at rest, retracted in flight. In breeding plumage bill blackish with yellow base, legs yellow, and gauzy white plumes on back. Non-breeding birds' bill yellow and legs blackish. **VOICE** Generally silent. Call harsh *krraah*. **DISTRIBUTION** In Egypt fairly common winter visitor to Delta and Valley and sporadically elsewhere, including on coasts. In Region in winter and on passage throughout. **HABITAT AND HABITS** In Region generally singly in freshwater, brackish, and marine habitats, including reedbeds, lakes, and riversides. Often with other herons and egrets, where white plumage distinguishes it from Grey and Purple Herons (p. 32); Little Egret (above) much smaller with black bill.

Grey Heron ■ *Ardea cinerea* 95cm WS 185cm

DESCRIPTION Large grey heron. Adult grey above with white underparts, streaked dark down neck and breast. Crown and back of neck black. Juvenile duller and browner. Bill yellowish, and heavy, long, and pointed. Legs long and yellow-brown. In flight neck retracted and wings grey with black primaries and secondaries. **VOICE** Loud, grating *wa-aark*. **DISTRIBUTION** In Egypt localized resident and widespread winter visitor to Delta and Valley, Western Oases, Sinai, and all coasts. Widespread in Region in winter and on passage, and localized breeder on Gulf coast and Saudi. **HABITAT AND HABITS** Marine, brackish, and freshwater wetlands, including mangroves. Stalks prey in shallow water, often remaining motionless for long periods of time. Long legged and long necked, but can appear stocky and squat when hunched at rest.

Purple Heron ■ *Ardea purpurea* 80cm WS 135cm

Juvenile

DESCRIPTION Slim, rakish heron. Smaller and darker than Grey Heron (above). Dark grey-purple above with chestnut flanks and rump. Pale below. Neck slender, chestnut with dark streaks; blackish crown and cheek-stripe. In flight darker and neck much more angular than Grey's. **Goliath Heron** *A. goliath* much larger, with huge bill and no black on crown, on southern Red Sea coasts. **VOICE** As Grey's but less carrying. **DISTRIBUTION** In Egypt common on passage and scarce in winter in Delta and Valley across to northern Sinai. In Region mainly on passage with local breeding in western Arabia, northern Gulf, and Levant. Goliath very local in southwest Arabia and southeastern Egypt. **HABITAT AND HABITS** Wetlands including reedbeds and marshes and on coast. Generally sticks to cover and usually encountered when flushed.

Yellow-billed Stork ■ *Mycteria ibis* 100cm WS 160cm

DESCRIPTION Large African stork. Predominantly white (at close range pink fringes to wing-coverts) with black primaries and secondaries and tail (white in White Stork, p. 34). Juvenile duller than adult. Bill large, slightly downcurved, and orange-yellow. Bare red facial skin. Legs reddish-orange. Differs in flight from White by black tail and bill color. Flies with neck less straight and bill more 'droopy'. **VOICE** Largely silent. **DISTRIBUTION** African species but regular summer visitor to very south of Egypt on Lake Nasser. Elsewhere in Region very rare vagrant or escape. **HABITAT AND HABITS** On Lake Nasser, shallow waters, sandbanks, and lake shore. Feeds singly or in small flocks.

Black Stork ■ *Ciconia nigra* 100cm WS 180cm

DESCRIPTION Black version of White Stork (p. 34) but slightly smaller. Upperparts, head, neck, and breast black, heavily glossed green and violet in good light. Belly and undertail-coverts white. Bill long, large, and red. Legs and eye-ring red. Juvenile duller than adult. In flight neck extended and wings all black except for white triangle at base of underside. **VOICE** Silent away from nest. **DISTRIBUTION** Scarce on passage in Egypt. On passage in Levant south to eastern Arabia. A few winter in southern Arabia. In southern Arabia, breeding **Abdim's Stork** C. *abdimii* much smaller, with shorter bill, and white on back. **HABITAT AND HABITS** Wetlands, open farmland, irrigation canals, and sewage ponds. On the ground 'stately' like White, but on passage not in such large flocks, and generally singly.

Black Stork

Abdim's Stork

White Stork ▪ *Ciconia ciconia* 105cm WS 200cm

DESCRIPTION Large, black and white bird. Long-necked, and predominantly white with black back and flight feathers. Black lores with long, large red bill, dark tipped in juvenile. Legs long and red. In flight neck held extended. Differs from Common Crane (p. 52) by black and white wings and red bare parts. **VOICE** On nest bill clattering – otherwise silent. **DISTRIBUTION** Common on passage in Egypt and throughout Region. Local breeder in Levant. Often migrates in large flocks, but singles overwinter and occasionally over-summer. **HABITAT AND HABITS** Wetlands, open farmland, irrigation canals, sewage ponds, and watersides. Walks purposefully on the ground ('stately'). Migrates in large, wheeling flocks, especially at migration hubs such as Suez, Hurghada, and north and south Sinai. Flocks silent.

Glossy Ibis ▪ *Plegadis falcinellus* 65cm WS 90cm

DESCRIPTION Heron-like waterbird. Dark throughout; appears blackish but at close quarters dark ruddy-brown, glossed green on wings and with indistinct white streaks on head and neck in winter. Bill long, downcurved, and pinkish in summer, brown in winter. In flight short tailed, and with neck extended and long legs projecting. **VOICE** Generally silent. Grunting at breeding colonies. **DISTRIBUTION** In Egypt fairly common on passage and less so in winter. Possible breeder in Delta. On passage throughout Region with some wintering. Local breeder in Levant. **HABITAT AND HABITS** Freshwater margins, marshes, and reedbeds. Singly or in small groups, often with heron or egret species. Nests colonially on the ground, less frequently in trees. Often flies in line, and flight often interspersed with long glides.

Eurasian Spoonbill ■ *Platalea leucorodia* 85cm WS 120cm

DESCRIPTION Egret-like waterbird. Long necked, long legged, and white throughout; in summer has nape-plumes and yellowish on lower parts. Bill broad and spatulate; black with yellow tip. Looks slim and slightly downcurved in profile. Legs blackish. In flight short tailed, with neck extended and legs projecting. **VOICE** Silent. **DISTRIBUTION** In Egypt scarce in winter and on passage in Delta and Valley, Western Oases, and coasts. Breeding resident on Red Sea islands. Elsewhere breeds along Arabian Red Sea coast and northern Gulf. Widespread on passage and in winter. **HABITAT AND HABITS** Expanses of shallow water (fresh or saline), estuaries, and mudflats. Breeds on offshore islands, often with mangroves. Superficially heron-like, but stance more horizontal and feeding action very different.

Greater Flamingo ■
Phoenicopterus roseus 130cm WS 150cm

DESCRIPTION Unmistakable. Tall, very long-legged and long-necked waterbird. Adult pinkish-white throughout with deep pink on wings. Bill large and sharply angled; reddish-pink, tipped black. Legs deep pink. Juvenile duller and greyer. In flight long neck outstretched, with carmine coverts and black flight feathers. **VOICE** Honking, much like geese. **DISTRIBUTION** In Egypt regular in winter and on passage in small to large flocks on northern lakes, Qarun, Siwa, and so on. Also on coast with individuals occasionally in summer; may breed. In Region widespread on passage and in winter, and very local breeder in Arabia. **HABITAT AND HABITS** Coastal lagoons, salt flats, and shallow lakes. Generally in flocks where, at a distance, birds can appear white, but note bill shape and leg color. Bright pink striking in flight.

Honey Buzzard ■ *Pernis apivorus* 52–59cm WS 120–140cm
(European Honey Buzzard)

Honey Buzzard

Crested Honey Buzzard

DESCRIPTION Superficially *Buteo*-like, but note proportionately smaller head and longer neck and tail. Variable brown above, from dark through rufous to pale. Head often grey. Eye has yellow iris. Underparts generally pale and barred. Tail rather long, banded, and with broad terminal band. In flight long winged, without clear carpal patch and rather extended neck. Soars on flat wings (slightly raised in Common Buzzard, p. 41). Differs from very similar, rare **Crested Honey Buzzard** *P. ptilorhynchus* by lack of sixth primary 'finger'. **VOICE** Silent on passage. **DISTRIBUTION** In Egypt mainly in east and Sinai on passage. In Region widespread throughout on passage only, though scarce in eastern Arabia. **HABITAT AND HABITS** On passage anywhere, but frequently migrates, often in large congregations, along migration corridors.

Black-winged Kite ■ *Elanus caeruleus* 31–36cm WS 76–88cm
(Black-shouldered Kite)

DESCRIPTION Small pale raptor. Adult blue-grey above with black 'shoulders', white face, and pale grey crown. Pure white below. Rather owl faced, with large, 'glaring' eyes with red iris. Legs short and yellow. In flight note short, square-ended tail and broad, pointed wings, grey with large black covert-patch and from below on wing-tips. Juvenile tinged brown on crown and breast and with scaly back. **VOICE** Generally silent – call piercing *chee-ark*. **DISTRIBUTION** In Egypt common resident throughout Delta and Valley and Fayoum. In Region very local resident confined to southwestern Arabia. **HABITAT AND HABITS** Open country with trees and farmland. Often perches on telephone and power wires. Hovers, where told from Common Kestrel (p. 46) by very white appearance, short tail, and broad wings with black.

Black Kite ■ *Milvus migrans* 48–58cm WS 130–155cm

DESCRIPTION Slim dark raptor. Adult dull, dark brown throughout with greyer head, sometimes markedly pale, and slightly forked tail. Juvenile has dark mask and pale tips to coverts. Bill small, and dark with yellow base. Legs yellow. In flight note tail with shallow fork, wings with deep fingers, and little pale on primaries. **Yellow-billed Kite** M. m. *aegyptius*, sometimes considered separate species, has more rufous underparts and all-yellow bill. **VOICE** Querulous mew and *pee-e-e-e*. **DISTRIBUTION** In Egypt Yellow-billed local resident in Delta and Valley. Other races widespread on passage. In Region local summer breeder in Levant and widespread throughout on passage. Yellow-billed resident in southeast Arabia. **HABITAT AND HABITS**. Open country, farmland, watersides, towns, villages, and rubbish tips. Even in central Cairo.

Black Kite

Yellow-billed Kite

Egyptian Vulture ■ *Neophron percnopterus* 55–65cm WS 155–170cm

DESCRIPTION Thin-billed, black and white vulture. Adult dirty white throughout with black flight feathers. Head proportionately small with shaggy crest, and bare facial skin bright yellow. Bill slender and hook tipped; yellow with black tip. In flight note long white, wedge-shaped tail. From below white with black primaries and secondaries – like White Stork (p. 34) but short necked and with yellow bare parts. Juvenile has same silhouette but dull brown throughout. **VOICE** Generally silent. **DISTRIBUTION** In Egypt, fairly common on passage and scarce breeder particularly in Valley, Eastern Desert, and Sinai. In Region summer breeder in Levant and Naqab. Resident in eastern and southern Arabia, Oman, and Gulf. Widespread on passage. **HABITAT AND HABITS** Mountains, wadis, and gorges. Also more open country and around rubbish tips in towns and villages.

Eurasian Griffon Vulture ■ *Gyps fulvus* 95–105cm WS 245–270cm

(Griffon Vulture)

DESCRIPTION Enormous vulture. Adult uniform buff-brown above with darker flight feathers. Pale brown below. White ruff. Head and neck have white down, often soiled. Heavy yellowish bill. In flight buff-brown, including back and rump, with darker primaries and secondaries and greater coverts tipped pale. Tail short, dark, and rounded. Flight

silhouette has distinct bulge to secondaries and deep fingers. Immature has brown ruff and grey bill. **VOICE** Unmusical hissing and grunting at carcasses. **DISTRIBUTION** In Egypt uncommon on passage mainly in Eastern Desert and Sinai. In Region very local resident in Levant, Naqab, and eastern Arabia. More widespread on passage and in winter. **HABITAT AND HABITS** Mountainous country with cliffs and ridges. Gregarious, breeding in colonies and assembling at carcasses.

Lappet-faced Vulture ■ *Torgos tracheliotus* 100–112cm WS 250–290cm

DESCRIPTION Enormous vulture. Adult huge; uniform blackish-brown above. Dark below with pale breast-sides, flanks and undertail-coverts streaked dark. Head and neck naked with pinkish pale skin and shaggy, dark brown ruff and hindneck. Bill massive. In

flight shows broad dark wings with pale line on underwing-coverts and short tail. Flight silhouette has slight bulge to secondaries and deep fingers. Immature more uniformly dark, with blue-grey facial skin. **VOICE** Generally silent. **DISTRIBUTION** In Egypt now confined to southern Eastern Desert, where breeds. Uncommon in central and south Arabia and southern Gulf, including Oman. Naqab population at best very rare. **HABITAT AND HABITS** Desert and semi-desert mountains and foothills, wadis, and gorges. Solitary or in pairs, although small flocks at carcasses where dominant.

Short-toed Eagle ▪ *Circaetus gallicus* 62–69cm WS 162–178cm
(Short-toed Snake Eagle)

DESCRIPTION Large pale eagle. Adult fairly uniform grey-brown above, including head and breast. Underparts sharply delineated from breast, whitish and coarsely barred. Unfeathered tarsi. Head proportionately large; rather owl-like with yellow eyes. In flight shows long, broad wings, evenly barred below and lacking dark carpal patches of Osprey (p. 45). Tail square ended, with three evenly spaced bars. Soars on flat wings; also hovers. Juvenile less strongly marked, especially below. **VOICE** Disyllabic whistling *kee-yo*. **DISTRIBUTION** In Egypt on passage in east and Sinai, where has bred. In Region summer breeder through Levant and Naqab. Patchy breeder in Arabia, where may be resident. Otherwise widespread on passage. **HABITAT AND HABITS** Semi-deserts, foothills, rocky slopes, and open plains with trees. Elsewhere on passage. Snake specialist.

Western Marsh Harrier ▪ *Circus aeruginosus* 48–55cm WS 115–130cm
(Marsh Harrier)

DESCRIPTION Large dark harrier. Male has chocolate-brown back and mantle, pale buff head, neck, and shoulders, and pale grey wings and tail. Underparts brown and streaked. In flight note black wing-tips and pale grey rump. Female larger, appearing mainly dark brown bar pale buff crown, forehead, and throat. In flight differs from Black Kite (p. 37) by rounded tail and pale head. **VOICE** Vocal when breeding. Alarm *keck-ek-ek-ek …* **DISTRIBUTION** In Egypt uncommon in winter in Delta and northern lakes. More widespread on passage. In Region very local breeder in northern Levant; formerly more widespread. Widespread throughout in winter and on passage. **HABITAT AND HABITS** Marshes, reedbeds, riversides, and damp farmland. Coasts over marshland in buoyant flight, with wings held in shallow 'V'.

Pallid Harrier ■ *Circus macrourus* 40–50cm WS 97–118cm

DESCRIPTION Male very pale blue-grey above and white below. In flight note black limited to narrow wedge on primaries. Rump white. Female similar to same-sized female Montagu's Harrier (below), being dull grey-brown above with pale underparts with dark streaks. Shares Montagu's rather owl-like facial pattern, but has clearer light collar and in

flight note more uniformly grey-brown above with dark secondary coverts below. VOICE Generally silent. Female utters thin whistle. DISTRIBUTION In Egypt rather scarce on passage, mostly in east including Sinai. Also winters in Valley and Delta. In Region widespread but scarce throughout in winter and on passage. HABITAT AND HABITS Grassland, steppes, farmland, and semi-desert. On migration also coastal marshes. Male distinctive if well seen. Female and juvenile compare to Montagu's.

Female (left); male (right)

Montagu's Harrier ■ *Circus pygargus* 39–50cm WS 96–116cm

DESCRIPTION Slim harrier. Male blue-grey above, darker than Pallid Harrier (above), with blue-grey head and breast fading to pale belly and flanks thinly streaked brown. In flight note long, slender wings, black band on secondaries, and extensive black wing-tips.

Female similar to female Pallid. Similar **Hen Harrier** C. *cyaneus* larger, broader winged, and more robust, with male lacking black band on secondaries. VOICE Normally quiet but *chiter chit-it-it-it* … when alarmed. DISTRIBUTION In Egypt fairly scarce on passage in east and Sinai. Absent in winter. In Region widespread throughout on passage. Rare in winter in southern Arabia. HABITAT AND HABITS Generally open country, marshes, and farmland. Also semi-deserts on passage. Smallest, slimmest harrier, often seen cruising with wings in shallow 'V'.

Eurasian Sparrowhawk ■ *Accipiter nisus* 29–41cm WS 58–80cm
(Sparrowhawk)

DESCRIPTION Small, broad-winged raptor. Dark slate-grey above. Smaller male has rufous cheeks and breast, and rufous barring on pale belly. Larger female lacks rufous, pale, barred brown-grey below, and has pale supercilium. Slender yellow legs. In flight note long, dark-banded tail and barred underwing. On passage similar **Levant Sparrowhawk** *A. brevipes* male has grey cheeks, unbarred tail, and plain underwing, and female has rufous barring. **VOICE** Largely silent outside breeding. **DISTRIBUTION** In Egypt widespread on passage, with some wintering in Delta, Valley, and Sinai. In Region local resident in Levant. Widespread in winter and on passage throughout. **HABITAT AND HABITS** Woodland and wood margins. On passage anywhere, but often migrates along migration corridors. Levant often in large flocks.

Eurasian Sparrowhawk   *Levant Sparrowhawk*

Common Buzzard ■ *Buteo buteo* 48–56cm WS 110–130cm

DESCRIPTION Medium-sized, broad-winged raptor. Variable; most numerous race in Region is 'Steppe Buzzard' *B. b. vulpinus*. Rather plain brown above, varying from dark through grey-brown to reddish-rufous, often with paler breast-band and eyebrow. Underparts variable, normally barred or streaked. Bill yellow with dark tip. In flight note plain rufous tail with narrow dark terminal band (absent in juvenile). From below note contrasting dark coverts or more rufous, with small, discreet dark carpal patch. **VOICE** Rather tremulous mew. **DISTRIBUTION** In Egypt common on passage especially in Sinai and Eastern Desert and Nile corridor. In Region very local breeder in Levant. Widespread on passage throughout. Rare in winter. **HABITAT AND HABITS** Woodland and treed hillsides. On passage anywhere but frequently migrates, often in large congregations, along migration corridors.

Steppe Buzzard   *Common Buzzard*

Long-legged Buzzard ■ *Buteo rufinus* 60–66cm WS 130–155cm

DESCRIPTION Very like 'Steppe Buzzard' *B. b. vulpinus*, but larger and longer winged. Variable, from dark through rufous to pale, but overall fairly uniform brown with paler

head and breast with darker belly and trousers; in race *cirtensis* more rufous. In flight note plain rufous tail grading to whitish rump and no black band. From below distinct carpal patch black, especially in pale birds. **VOICE** Mew as 'Steppe's'. **DISTRIBUTION** In Egypt local breeder mainly in Sinai. More widespread, especially in east, on passage; a few winter. In Region resident over much of Levant to Naqab and patchily through Arabia and Gulf. Widespread in winter and on passage. **HABITAT AND HABITS** Breeds in mountains and semi-deserts. On passage as 'Steppe'. Often perches on the ground. Hovers.

Lesser Spotted Eagle ■ *Aquila pomarina* 55–65cm WS 143–168cm

DESCRIPTION Medium-sized dark eagle. Adult dark brown, paler on head and neck. Broad wings with shorter fingers than in other *Aquila* eagles and slim 'trousers' at rest.

Bill small, buzzard-like. From below coverts generally paler than densely barred flight feathers that appear uniform dark (barring clearer, more open in Steppe Eagle, opposite). Juvenile has prominent white tips to coverts and white trailing edge to wing. From above pale patch on primaries. **VOICE** Generally quiet on passage. **DISTRIBUTION** In Egypt fairly common on passage through Sinai and eastern part of the country. In Region on passage through Levant south to Naqab. **HABITAT AND HABITS** On passage in open country, often around wetlands. Migrates in flocks where main confusion is with larger Steppe.

Greater Spotted Eagle ■ *Aquila clanga* 59–69cm WS 155–180cm

DESCRIPTION Large, very dark eagle. Adult dark brown throughout, including neck and head. Broad winged with deep fingers. At rest shows fuller 'trousers' than Lesser Spotted Eagle (opposite). Bill moderately heavy. From below coverts generally as dark as flight feathers and no dark band on trailing edge. From above shows only diffuse pale primary patch. Juvenile dark and heavily spotted white (more so than Lesser Spotted). From below no pale bar or primary patch (see juvenile Steppe Eagle, below). **VOICE** Generally quiet on passage. **DISTRIBUTION** In Egypt rare winter visitor to Delta and also on passage in east. In Region on passage throughout but generally rare. A few winter. **HABITAT AND HABITS** Less open country than Lesser-spotted and Steppe. Often in vicinity of marshes and wetlands with woods.

Steppe Eagle ■ *Aquila nipalensis* 62–75cm WS 165–200cm

DESCRIPTION Large to very large; larger than very similar 'spotted eagles'. Adult dark brown throughout with long, broad wings, deeply fingered, and at rest shows heavy 'trousers'. Yellow gape extends back to rear of eye. From below, paler birds show dark carpal patch and dark trailing edge. Flight feathers have evenly spaced bars and from above pale primary patch. Immature has distinct pale margins to coverts forming pale bar across wing, and pale primary patch. Narrow pale base to tail. **VOICE** Generally silent. **DISTRIBUTION** Fairly common in Egypt on passage, particularly through Sinai and Eastern Desert. In Region widespread throughout on passage; rarer in winter. **HABITAT AND HABITS** Open country, plains, and semi-deserts. Also wetlands and hills. On migration in large concentrations.

Juvenile

Golden Eagle ■ *Aquila chrysaetos* 80–93cm WS 190–225cm

DESCRIPTION Very large, powerful eagle. Adult dark brown throughout, paler on wing-coverts, and with rusty-yellow on back of neck. Powerful bill, yellow with dark tip. In flight note paler upperwing-coverts. Below all dark, with paler flight feathers banded dark and with broad dark tips. Note curved rear edge to wing. Tail long and banded. Immature birds have white tail with broad dark terminal band and clear white patches on wing. **VOICE** Generally silent. Thin whistle recorded in flight. **DISTRIBUTION** In Egypt rare resident in northeastern Sinai. Scarce in winter, generally in east. In Region very local resident breeder in Levant and Arabia to southern Gulf and Oman. Some winter dispersal. **HABITAT AND HABITS** Mountains, barren or wooded, more open plains, and semi-deserts.

Booted Eagle ■ *Aquila pennata* 43–53cm WS 110–130cm

DESCRIPTION Small eagle with two color phases. Pale phase brown above with whitish underparts, including underwing-coverts, but darker head and neck. Dark phase has slightly

streaked dark rufous-brown to rufous underparts, and in flight note dark mid-wing bar and pale patch on upperwing. Tail square with sharp 'corners', plain or only lightly banded. Compared with buzzards note feathered tarsi at rest and more deeply fingered wings in flight. **VOICE** Quiet on passage, with buzzard-like mew recorded. **DISTRIBUTION** In Egypt, rather scarce passage migrant through Sinai, Eastern Desert to Valley. In Region very local breeder in northern Levant. Otherwise widespread on passage throughout, with a few wintering in Arabia. **HABITAT AND HABITS** Breeds in woodland. On passage more open country, semi-deserts, and scrub.

Bonelli's Eagle ■ *Aquila fasciatus* 58–68cm WS 145–165cm

DESCRIPTION Medium-large, slim, broad-winged eagle. Adult rather uniform grey-brown above with whitish patch on mantle. Underparts whitish-pale finely streaked dark. Powerful yellow bill with dark tip.

In flight note dark underwing with black carpal patch and wing-bar from below, very straight trailing edge to secondaries, and grey, square-ended tail with broad dark terminal band. Juvenile has plain rufous underparts and densely barred tail. **VOICE** Silent on passage. **DISTRIBUTION** In Egypt local resident breeder in south Sinai, more widespread after winter dispersal and passage. In Region patchily distributed, resident from southern Levant through Arabia and Gulf with some winter dispersal. **HABITAT AND HABITS** Breeds in rocky highlands and wooded hills, dispersing over more open country, including semi-deserts and desert margins.

Osprey ■ *Pandion haliaetus* 52–60cm WS 145–165cm

DESCRIPTION Medium-large raptor tied to water. Upperparts dark brown. White below. Head white with dark stripe through eye and down side of neck. Tail rather shortish, banded dark with broad terminal band. Wings long and markedly angled in flight. Legs and feet blue-grey. **VOICE** Vocal. Call loud *pee-ep*. **DISTRIBUTION** In Egypt breeds along Red Sea coast and Sinai, chiefly on offshore islands. Also inland on passage and in winter on Nile and lakes, for example Qarun. In Region widespread on passage, breeding on Arabian Gulf and Red Sea coasts. **HABITAT AND HABITS** Inland and coastal waters. In Region generally nests on the ground, often in loose colonies, for example in Egyptian Red Sea. Fishes over open water, hovering and plunging in after prey. Often perches prominently on masts, mangroves, and similar.

Common Kestrel ■ *Falco tinnunculus* 31–37cm WS 68–78cm

Common Kestrel   *Lesser Kestrel*

DESCRIPTION Small, long-winged, long-tailed falcon. Male has black-spotted chestnut upperparts and grey head with darker moustachial stripe. Underparts pale with dark spots. Tail grey with dark terminal band. Female larger, with brown head and barred brown tail. Claws dark. Summer visitor and migrant **Lesser Kestrel** F. *naumanni* male has unspotted mantle; female very similar to Common but claws pale. **VOICE** Urgent *kee kee kee kee*, particularly in spring. Also quavering trills. **DISTRIBUTION** In Egypt widespread resident throughout, including Western Oases but not true desert. Common resident over much of Region. Also on passage and winter visitor. **HABITAT AND HABITS** Open country, but also towns and villages; even central Cairo. Hunts for small birds, rodents, lizards, and large insects, often hovering.

Merlin ■ *Falco columbarius* 26–33cm WS 55–69cm

DESCRIPTION Smallest falcon, with stocky, 'heavy' silhouette. Male blue-grey above and on crown. Rusty on nape. Underparts rusty-orange, finely streaked dark and with white throat. Thin moustachial stripe. Tail grey with broad black terminal band. Female dark grey-brown above (race *pallidus* paler and more rufous) and buff, heavily streaked dark below. In flight note tail with five broad dark bars and barred primaries. **VOICE** Generally silent outside breeding. **DISTRIBUTION** In Egypt scarce winter visitor mainly to north including Delta, and more widespread on passage. In Region on passage through Levant to western Arabia and Gulf. Rare in winter. **HABITAT AND HABITS** Open country, semi-deserts, marshland, and farmland. Hunts mainly small birds low over the ground.

Hobby ■ *Falco subbuteo* 32–36cm WS 74–92cm

DESCRIPTION Dashing, medium-sized falcon. Adult dark slate-grey above with white cheeks and prominent black moustachial stripe. Pale, heavily and darkly streaked below with rufous-red thighs and undertail-coverts. In flight note pointed wings with barred underwing-coverts and relatively short tail. Light-phase **Eleonora's Falcon** *F. eleonorae*,

rare on passage, similar but larger, and rusty-brown streaked dark below, with dark underwing-coverts. **VOICE** Loud *kew, kew, kew* ... **DISTRIBUTION** In Egypt widespread but uncommon on passage. May breed in Sinai. In Region local summer breeder in Levant. Widespread on passage throughout. **HABITAT AND HABITS** Open country with trees, farmland, and wetlands. Aerial. Fast and agile, hunting for small birds, and insects such as large dragonflies, caught and eaten on the wing.

Juvenile

Sooty Falcon ■ *Falco concolor* 32–38cm WS 78–90cm

DESCRIPTION Slender, long-winged falcon. Uniform slate-grey throughout with darker primaries and on tail. Cere, eye-ring, legs and feet yellow. Wing-tip reaches tail-tip when perched. Sexes alike. Juvenile has paler feather margins above and streaked dark below. Passage male **Red-footed Falcon** *F. vespertinus* similar but with red thighs and vent. Female paler with yellowish head. **VOICE** Similar to Common Kestrel's (opposite). **DISTRIBUTION** In Egypt summer breeder along Red Sea coast. Also Eastern Desert,

Western Desert, and Sinai. Largely coastal summer breeder in Arabia, but also inland north to Jordan. Widespread on passage. **HABITAT AND HABITS** Bird of rocky deserts and gorges, rocky sea coasts, and offshore islands. Preys largely on birds and breeds late to take advantage of autumn migration. Nests singly or in colonies.

Sooty Falcon

Red-footed Falcon

Lanner Falcon ■ *Falco biarmicus* 43–53cm WS 95–115cm

DESCRIPTION Large, rather narrow-winged falcon. Adult upperparts blue-grey (juvenile browner); underparts pale and spotted. Head buffish with dark, slim moustachial stripe. At rest wing-tips reach tail-tip; tail evenly barred. In flight pale below with streaked coverts forming darker band. Rare **Saker Falcon** *F. cherrug* larger and heavier, tawny brown with pale head and thin moustachial stripe. **VOICE** At breeding sites *kra-ee kra-ee kra-ee*. **DISTRIBUTION** In Egypt, resident breeder over much of Valley, southern Delta, Western Oases, Eastern Desert, and Sinai. Localized breeder in Levant and Arabia. Widespread throughout Region on passage. **HABITAT AND HABITS** Hills, wadis, deserts, and open country. Preys largely on birds caught in open flight or stoop (slower than Peregrine Falcon, below).

Peregrine Falcon ■ *Falco peregrinus* 38–51cm WS 89–120cm

DESCRIPTION Large, powerful falcon. Sexes similar but female considerably larger than male. Slate-grey above; white, barred dark below. Dark head with broad moustachial stripe and white throat. Flight silhouette cigar shaped with pointed, broad-based wings and rather short tail. **Barbary Falcon** *F. pelegrinoides* smaller, paler and browner, with rufous on nape, sometimes considered conspecific. **VOICE** Mainly silent. Call harsh *rek rek rek …* **DISTRIBUTION** Widespread on passage and in winter throughout region. Barbary localized breeding resident in Delta east to Sinai and throughout Arabia north to Jordan. In Egypt, Barbary localized breeding. **HABITAT AND HABITS** Open habitats, mountains, and cliffs. Also sea-coast sand marshes; even cities (Cairo, Alexandria). Barbary breeds in mountains, desert wadis, and semi-deserts. Hunts prey the size of pigeons and partridges, often stooping at immense speed from a great height.

Peregrine Falcon

Barbary Falcon

Water Rail ▪ *Rallus aquaticus* 26cm

DESCRIPTION Like a large crake but slimmer and longer billed. Upperparts mottled dark brown with pale feather margins. Cheeks, face, and underparts slaty-grey, barred black and white on flanks. Undertail white. Bill long, slender, slightly decurved, and red. Flight with dull reddish legs dangling. **VOICE**

Vocal. Loud *koop koop koop* … including at night. Persistent. Also grunts and loud squeal. **DISTRIBUTION** In Egypt uncommon breeding resident in Delta and North Coast. More widespread in winter. Local resident in Gulf, northern Arabia, and northern Levant, but widespread on passage and in winter. **HABITAT AND HABITS** Secretive, in dense vegetation in reedbeds, ponds, irrigation canals, and ditches. Laterally 'thin as a rail', creeping through undergrowth, where best located by white undertail or if flushed.

Spotted Crake ▪ *Porzana porzana* 23cm

DESCRIPTION Compact, short-billed version of Water Rail (above). Brown upperparts with beige feather margins and densely spotted white. Underparts grey, spotted white and with flanks barred black and white. Undertail-coverts buff. Bill short, and yellow with red base. Legs greenish-yellow. Similar **Little Crake** *P. parva* and **Baillon's Crake** *P. pusilla* both rare in Egypt and Region; smaller and less spotted. **VOICE** Long, repeated whistle, often delivered at night. **DISTRIBUTION** In Egypt uncommon winter visitor to Delta and Valley. On passage elsewhere. In Region very local summer breeder in northern Gulf; on passage throughout, some wintering. **HABITAT AND HABITS** Secretive inhabitant of densely vegetated swamps and marshes, dank water margins, and irrigation ditches. Elusive, creeping in vegetation. When flushed, often has legs dangling.

Spotted Crake

Little Crake

Corncrake ▪ *Crex crex* 28cm

DESCRIPTION Like unrelated Quail (p. 21), but much slimmer and more elongated. Slim, long-necked crake. Tortoiseshell above, dark brown with beige feather margins. Head, throat, and breast grey (beiger in female) with brown on crown and from behind eye. Short, pinkish bill. Legs pinkish. In flight note bright chestnut-brown wings, especially coverts, and legs often dangling. **VOICE** Onomatopoeic *crex crex* but mostly silent on

passage. **DISTRIBUTION** Uncommon on passage in Egypt, especially along North Coast. In Region widespread throughout on passage but rarely encountered. **HABITAT AND HABITS** Less tied to water and moist habitat than other crakes. Pasture, grassland, and agricultural areas. Skulking and shy, and most often seen when flushed. In Egypt most frequent in north Sinai in autumn but has declined everywhere.

Common Moorhen ▪ *Gallinula chloropus* 31cm
(Moorhen, Common Gallinule)

DESCRIPTION All-dark relative of rails. Adult dark slate-grey throughout, with white line along each flank and white undertail-coverts divided by vertical black stripe. Face-plate red. Bill red with yellow tip. Legs yellow-green. Juvenile dull brown with white flank-line and undertail. **VOICE** Noisy. Harsh barks and grunts. Sharp *kek* and also

persistent *krrekk-krrekk-krrekk*. **DISTRIBUTION** In Egypt common resident, and in winter in Delta and Valley, Western Oases, and North Coast. Common, localized breeder throughout Region, more widespread in winter and on passage. **HABITAT AND HABITS** Freshwater wetlands, rivers, lakes, ponds, and irrigation canals. In thick vegetation, where best located by voice. Also swims out in the open with jerky action. On land walks deliberately on large feet.

Purple Swamphen ■ *Porphyrio porphyrio* 48cm
(Purple Gallinule)

DESCRIPTION Like a large purple Common
Moorhen (opposite). Glossy dark purple-blue
throughout; greenish back in *madagascariensis* in
Egypt and paler headed in east of Region. White
undertail-coverts. Red face-plate and outsize bill.
Large feet and red legs. In flight all dark with
dangling feet and legs. Juvenile greyer and duller
than adult. **VOICE** Vocal. Loud *chuk*, sharper
tschak tschak, as well as assorted clucks, honks, and
brays. **DISTRIBUTION** Egyptian *madagascariensis*
common breeding resident in Delta and Valley.
Also in Fayoum and northern lakes. Local breeding
resident in northeastern Syria and Gulf. **HABITAT
AND HABITS** Wetlands with extensive
cover, reedbeds, riversides, lakes, and canals.
Unmistakable if seen well, but secretive and most
often seen disappearing into thick cover, when size
and undivided white undertail-coverts distinct.

Eurasian Coot ■ *Fulica atra* 40cm
(Coot)

DESCRIPTION Stocky, all-black waterbird. Duck-like on the water but blunt ended.
Black/dark grey throughout. At rest superficially like stocky, less angular Common
Moorhen (opposite) but with no white in plumage and white face-plate and bill. Red
iris. Legs greenish and lobed toes. Almost tailless in flight. **VOICE** Noisy. Variety of
calls, including loud *krook*,
nasal trumpeting and alarm
pittz. **DISTRIBUTION** In Egypt
scarce breeding resident in Delta,
wintering throughout Delta,
Valley, and elsewhere. Localized
breeding resident throughout
Region, much more widespread in
winter and on passage. **HABITAT
AND HABITS** Areas of open
fresh water, mainly larger lakes,
and reservoirs, and in winter also
saltwater. In winter in large flocks,
often with ducks and grebes, but
white face-plate diagnostic.

Common Crane ■ *Grus grus* 115cm WS 230cm

DESCRIPTION Large, heron-like waterbird. Tall, elegant, and largely grey throughout, with long, white-backed black neck. Red on crown hard to see. Adult shows large bustle of dark-tipped grey feathers at rest. Bill short and pale. Legs dark. In flight wings uniform grey below, above black primaries – neck extended. **VOICE** Vocal, with far-carrying, deep, sonorous *kkrrro* in flight. **DISTRIBUTION** In Egypt fairly common on passage throughout, sometimes in large flocks. Elsewhere in Region also widespread on passage, with a very few overwintering. **HABITAT AND HABITS** Wetlands, marshes, and farmland. Migrating flocks along Nile Delta and Valley often heard before seen. In flight similar to White Stork (p. 34) but not black and white and lacks red of bare parts. Elegant on the ground.

Macqueen's Bustard ■ *Chlamydotis macqueenii* 60cm WS 150cm

DESCRIPTION Size of large, long-tailed domestic fowl. Upperparts pale brown, heavily vermiculated with black and grey. Long neck pale grey with black stripe down side. Breast grey and belly white. Black and white crest. Female smaller and plainer than male. Bill rather long, and pointed. Legs strong and yellowish-grey. In flight broad winged with clear fingers. Flight feathers black with large white patch on primaries. **VOICE** Largely silent. **DISTRIBUTION** In Egypt rare winter visitor to Eastern Desert; possibly resident in

Sinai. Similar **Houbara Bustard** *C. undulata* rare in Egypt's Western Desert. In Region local resident in Naqab and northern Arabia, and southern Arabia. Rare in winter and on passage throughout. **HABITAT AND HABITS** Semi-deserts, stony plains, and cultivation. Shy. Widely hunted and now much reduced over entire range.

Macqueen's Bustard   *Houbara Bustard*

Greater Painted Snipe ■ *Rostratula benghalensis* 25cm WS 52cm
(Painted Snipe)

DESCRIPTION Secretive, distinctive wader. Female very dark above. Head, neck, and upper breast deep chestnut with white eye-stripe. Underparts clean white with white line extending around corner of wing. Male brownish-green above with dark barring, and grey-brown on head, neck, and breast with beige eye-stripe. Underparts white with beige 'braces' extending over back. Bill pale and slender with drooping tip. Legs pale yellowish, projecting beyond tail in flight. **VOICE** Quiet, but female utters low *koot*. **DISTRIBUTION** Confined to Egypt, where resident in Delta and a few outlying areas such as Wadi Natrun and Fayoum. Vagrant in Levant and Arabia. **HABITAT AND HABITS** Densely vegetated marshes, ponds, irrigation canals, and ditches. Crepuscular; best seen at dusk. When flushed note broad, very rounded wings.

Male

Female

Eurasian Oystercatcher ■ *Haematopus ostralegus* 42cm WS 83cm
(Oystercatcher)

DESCRIPTION Large, chunky black and white wader. Pied; black above including head and chest; in winter has white chin-band. All white below. Long, straight, bright red bill and red orbital ring. Legs pinkish. In flight black with white back, rump and black-tipped white tail. Broad white wing-bar. **VOICE** Vocal. Loud, carrying peep in flight and shrill *klee klee klee klee …* when agitated. **DISTRIBUTION** In Egypt scarce winter visitor

and on passage to all coasts. Less common inland on lake shores. In Region in winter and on passage throughout. **HABITAT AND HABITS** Mainly coastal on rocky and sandy coasts, mudflats, and estuaries. Less often inland on larger waterbodies. Often singly, in pairs or in small flocks. Feeds with bill aimed down, prodding at mud or shellfish beds.

Black-winged Stilt ■ *Himantopus himantopus* 36cm WS 72cm

DESCRIPTION Extraordinarily long pink legs. Male has black upperparts and black back to head and neck; duskier in winter. White face, neck, and underparts. Female browner above with less dark on head and neck. Bill needle-thin and straight. Legs very long and

pink. In flight white with black wings. **VOICE** Call ringing *ki ki ki ki* or *kee-ak*. **DISTRIBUTION** In Egypt probable breeder in Delta. Widespread in winter and on passage. In Region localized resident breeder in Syria, southern Levant, and all coasts of Arabia. Widespread in winter and on passage throughout. **HABITAT AND HABITS** Coasts, estuaries, and lagoons. Also inland on brackish and freshwater lakes and ponds. Wades through water, often in company of other waders, when unmistakeable.

Pied Avocet ▪ *Recurvirostra avosetta* 44cm WS 75cm

(Avocet)

DESCRIPTION Elegant black and white wader. Largely white with black down sides of back, coverts and primaries, and on head, nape, and back of neck. Bill black, long, very slender, and strongly upturned. Legs long and pale blue. In flight pied with all-white tail and rump and legs projecting. **VOICE** Call loud *kloop kloop kloop* … **DISTRIBUTION** In Egypt in winter and on passage on all coasts. Less common inland. Possible rare breeder. In Region in winter and on passage throughout. Localized breeder in Levant, Gulf, and eastern Arabia. **HABITAT AND HABITS** Mainly coastal on estuaries, mudflats, sandbanks, and lagoons. Also inland on large areas of shallow water, especially saline water. Feeds walking through the water, sweeping distinctive bill from side to side.

Crab Plover ▪ *Dromas ardeola* 39cm WS 77cm

DESCRIPTION Distinctive, large black and white wader. Largely white above with black back and primaries. Head white with very large, heavy black bill. In winter and juvenile more streaked above. Legs long and blue-grey. In flight very black and white, with legs projecting beyond all-white tail and head tucked in. **VOICE** Noisy at breeding colonies, with loud *chuk-chuk-chuk* … Alarm call loud *wedd-dek*. **DISTRIBUTION** In Egypt restricted to southern Red Sea coast but not proven to breed. Elsewhere in Region localized resident breeder along Arabian Red Sea coast and Gulf coast with non-breeding dispersal to all Arabian coasts. **HABITAT AND HABITS** Strictly coastal on rocky and sandy shores, mudflats, and reefs. Colonial breeder unique among waders in nesting in burrows. Immatures often seen accompanying parent.

Eurasian Stone Curlew ▪ *Burhinus oedicnemus* 42cm WS 81cm

DESCRIPTION Distinctive, cryptic, streaky brown wader. Streaked brown above with white belly. At rest shows black-bordered white wing-bar. Short, rather heavy bill, yellow

with dark tip. Large, 'staring' yellow eyes. Legs yellow with prominent tarsi. In flight wings black and white above, pale below. **VOICE** In nocturnal display *klurlee, klurlee, klurlee* … Also *koolee* call. **DISTRIBUTION** In Egypt common resident throughout Valley, across North Coast and north Sinai. In Region summer breeder in Levant south to Naqab. Widespread throughout on passage and in winter. **HABITAT AND HABITS** Semi-deserts, plains, agricultural areas, and open scrub. Walks slowly and deliberately, often 'freezing'.

Senegal Thick-knee ▪ *Burhinus senegalensis* 38cm WS 78cm

DESCRIPTION Large, rather cryptically colored wader. Streaked brown above with white belly. Pale greyish wing-panel rather than bar. Short, rather heavy bill, heavier

than Eurasian Stone Curlew's (above). Large, 'staring' yellow eyes. Legs yellow with prominent tarsi. In flight wings black and white above, pale below. Pale in flight, with rather pointed wings. **VOICE** Far-carrying, mournful *pvi pvi pvi pvi* … rising to crescendo, then falling. Characteristic sound at night over much of Egyptian range. **DISTRIBUTION** In Region confined to Egypt's Nile Delta and Valley. **HABITAT AND HABITS** Open ground generally close to water, lakes and riversides, and irrigation ditches. Unobtrusive by day; active at night, attracting attention by call. Can be found in urban areas even in central Cairo.

Cream-colored Courser ■ *Cursorius cursor* 26cm WS 54cm

DESCRIPTION Elegant, plover-like wader of bare, dry terrain. Pale sandy-beige throughout with paler to white underparts. Head delicately patterned with blue-grey nape and black-bordered white supercilia that meet behind head. Bill slender and curved. Legs long and white. In flight note black primaries and entirely black underwing. **VOICE** Rather soft *kwwett*. **DISTRIBUTION** In Egypt resident breeder across North Coast, Delta and Valley margins, Eastern Desert, Red Sea coast, and Sinai. Summer visitor to much of Levant and localized resident in Arabia, including much of Gulf. Widespread on passage and in winter. **HABITAT AND HABITS** Semi-deserts, both sandy and stony, desert margins, grassland, and dry coastal plains. Singly or in pairs, small flocks characteristically running and freezing on the ground.

Collared Pratincole ■ *Glareola pratincola* 25cm WS 63cm

DESCRIPTION More tern-like than wader. Slim and short necked. Upperparts uniform olive-brown with slender dark primaries. Throat creamy-white, bordered black. Tail deeply forked. Bill short with red base. Legs short and dark. In flight note long, pointed wings with reddish-brown underwing-coverts and white trailing edge. Much rarer **Black-winged Pratincole** G. *nordmanni* very similar, with black underwing-coverts; no white margin. **VOICE** Abrupt *kekk* and tern-like chattering. **DISTRIBUTION** In Egypt local summer breeder in Delta and Fayoum. More widespread on passage. In Region very localized summer breeder in Levant and coastal Arabia; much more widespread on passage. **HABITAT AND HABITS** Breeding colonies on dry mudflats and grassland. Also plains, drier marshland, and saltpans. Very aerial, hawking insects like large marsh tern, often in flocks.

Little Ringed Plover ■ *Charadrius dubius* 16cm WS 45cm

DESCRIPTION Very similar to Ringed Plover (below), with same basic pattern but differs as follows. Appears slimmer and longer billed. In summer white behind black forecrown, dark bill, and prominent yellow orbital ring. In winter duller and with pale orbital ring.

Legs longer and pinkish. In flight no white wing-bar. **VOICE** Loud *pee-ew* given in flight. Harsher alarm call, *pree*. **DISTRIBUTION** In Egypt scarce summer breeder in Delta and northern Valley. More widespread on passage. In Region summer breeder in Levant, eastern Arabia, and Gulf. On passage throughout with a few wintering in southern Arabia. **HABITAT AND HABITS** Breeds by fresh water on riversides, sandbanks, and lake shores. Also on coast in winter. Generally singly or in pairs.

Ringed Plover ■ *Charadrius hiaticula* 19cm WS 52cm
(Common Ringed Plover)

DESCRIPTION Rather squat, short-billed plover. Upperparts uniform grey-brown. Head has black mask and forecrown, and complete white collar, throat, forehead, and supercilium. No distinct eye-ring. Underparts white with complete black breast-band. Short orange bill with black tip. In winter black markings replaced by dark brown and bill all dark. Legs

orange to yellow. In flight shows clear white wing-bar. **VOICE** Calls include *peep* and two-syllable *poo-eep*. **DISTRIBUTION** In Egypt fairly common winter visitor to northern and Red Sea coasts. Also inland. In Region in winter and on passage widespread throughout. **HABITAT AND HABITS** All types of rocky and sandy coasts, mangroves, and lagoons. Also inland lakes, mudflats, and sandbanks.

Kittlitz's Plover ▪ *Charadrius pecuarius* 14cm WS 42cm

DESCRIPTION Small, dark 'ringed plover'. Rather dark, mottled brown above with brown crown. Distinctive head pattern with white supercilium around to broad white nape. Black mask, lores, and across forecrown. White forehead and throat. Underparts washed pale orange-buff. Head markings duller in winter. Fairly long, dark legs and thin dark bill. In flight toes project beyond tail (they do not in Kentish Plover, below). **VOICE** Calls include *chik* and *drrr*. **DISTRIBUTION** Within Region this African species is an Egypt specialty. Resident breeder in Delta and Wadi Natrun and Fayoum. Vagrant elsewhere in Region. **HABITAT AND HABITS** Shallow freshwater and saline lakes, lagoons, flats, and pondsides. Very cryptic on the ground due to mottled upperparts and best located by movement.

Kentish Plover ▪ *Charadrius alexandrinus* 16cm WS 44cm

DESCRIPTION Small, pale 'ringed plover'. Summer adult pale sandy-beige above with white collar, rufous nape, and pale brown crown. Black through eye and on forecrown, with white forehead and supercilium. White underparts with incomplete black breast-band. In winter duller. Thin black bill and black legs. In flight note white wing-bar and sides to dark tail. **VOICE** Calls include soft whistle, and in flight *bip* or *twit*. **DISTRIBUTION** In Egypt common resident in Delta, Sinai, and northern Red Sea. Also winter visitor and on passage throughout. In Region widespread resident breeder on Mediterranean and Arabian coasts including Gulf. In winter and on passage throughout. **HABITAT AND HABITS** Sandy, muddy and shingle coastlines, estuaries, and lagoons. Inland, lakes, and freshwater and saline lagoons.

Breeding

Greater Sand Plover ■ *Charadrius leschenaultii* 24cm WS 56cm

DESCRIPTION Large, long-legged 'ringed plover'. Breeding adult has uniform brown upperparts and crown. Chestnut across forecrown, above eye to nape and breast-band. Black forecrown and through lores and eye, with white forehead and throat. In winter duller, browner. Bill long, pointed, and rather heavy. Legs long and yellow-green. Scarcer **Lesser Sand Plover** *C. mongolus* very similar in winter but smaller, with shorter bill and shorter, dark grey legs. **VOICE** Calls include trilling *trrr* and *huit huit huit* in flight. **DISTRIBUTION** In Egypt in winter along Mediterranean and Red Sea coasts with some inland; more widespread on passage. In Region patchy summer breeder in Levant and northern Gulf. On passage and in winter throughout. **HABITAT AND HABITS** Inland mudflats, sandbanks, and plains, but in winter largely coastal.

Lesser Sand Plover   *Greater Sand Plover (non-breeding)*

Caspian Plover ■ *Charadrius asiaticus* 20cm WS 58cm

DESCRIPTION Like sand plovers but slimmer, more elongated, and longer legged. Non-breeding uniform grey-brown above. Head pale grey-brown with broad cream-buff supercilium, forehead, and throat. Grey-brown breast-band and white underparts.

In summer has much whiter supercilium, and male has chestnut breast and narrow black breast-band. Bill dark, fine, and tapered. Fairly long grey-green legs. In flight slim winged with short white wing-bar, grey-brown rump, and feet projecting beyond tail. **VOICE** Short *chup* or *tyup* given in flight. **DISTRIBUTION** In Egypt rare on passage mainly to north and Sinai. In Region widespread but generally rare on passage in Arabia. Very rare in Levant. **HABITAT AND HABITS** Grassland, semi-deserts, plains, and also coasts.

Eurasian Dotterel ■ *Charadrius morinellus* 21cm WS 60cm

DESCRIPTION Rather brown plover. In summer plain grey-brown above to nape and upper breast. White crescent across chest. Below, chestnut with black belly. White face with bold white supercilium contrasting with blackish crown. In winter paler throughout and with more uniform orange-buff underparts and obscure pale crescent across chest. Slight dark bill. Greenish-yellow legs. In flight note pale buffish underwing; no white wing-bar or tail-tip. **VOICE** Dry *dryrrr* and *pwit*. **DISTRIBUTION** Scarce in Egypt on passage and in winter to Delta and Sinai. In Region some winter in Levant east to northern Gulf. Also on passage. **HABITAT AND HABITS** Breeds in mountains. On passage and in winter open plains, agricultural areas, and open farmland.

Pacific Golden Plover ■ *Pluvialis fulva* 23cm WS 66cm

DESCRIPTION Smaller and slimmer than Grey Plover (p. 62). In winter upperparts spangled with subdued yellow-gold. Underparts paler and dappled in spring, showing varying degrees of black. Bill straight and dark. Legs longish and dark, extending beyond tail in flight. Pale supercilium. Brownish underwings. Similar **Eurasian Golden Plover** *P. apricaria* larger, with proportionately shorter legs and bill, and whitish underwing. **VOICE** Soft *kru-it*. **DISTRIBUTION** Not in Egypt (where Eurasian is scarce winter visitor to north including Sinai). In Region regular in winter and on passage along Gulf and also southwest Arabia. Vagrant in Levant. **HABITAT AND HABITS** Coastal, on mudflats, beaches, and mangroves. Also farmland and grassland. Singly and in small flocks. Flight very rapid.

Pacific Golden Plover

Eurasian Golden Plover

Grey Plover ■ *Pluvialis squatarola* 28cm WS 77cm

DESCRIPTION Large, fairly rotund, big-headed plover. In winter upperparts grey, heavily mottled with darker grey and pale – 'colder' than golden plovers. Underparts whitish with mottled breast. Obscure pale supercilium. Bill dark and heavy for a plover. Legs dark. In spring has brighter upperparts and all-black face, breast, and belly. In flight, in all plumages note black 'wing-pits', bold white wing-bar, and white rump. VOICE Trisyllabic whistle, *dee-oo-weee*. DISTRIBUTION In Egypt fairly common in Delta and along coasts in winter and on passage. In Region on passage throughout. In winter mainly coastal. HABITAT AND HABITS Coastal flats, estuaries, and lagoons. Inland mainly on shallow lakes and wetlands. Generally singly.

Spur-winged Lapwing ■ *Vanellus spinosus* 27cm WS 75cm
(Spur-winged Plover)

DESCRIPTION Striking black and white lapwing. Upperparts pale grey-brown. Black breast, flanks, and tail with white rump and undertail-coverts. Black throat and hood with white cheeks. Short dark bill. Legs rather long and black. In flight very black and white with grey-brown coverts and back. VOICE Very vocal and noisy. Loud *pik pik* … delivered in flight and on the ground. DISTRIBUTION In Egypt widespread resident throughout Delta, Valley, and Fayoum, with dispersal elsewhere. In Region resident in Levant and eastern Arabia south to Yemen, again with dispersal. HABITAT AND HABITS Freshwater and saltwater marshes, open farmland, and irrigated areas, including golf courses, parks, playing fields, and similar. Makes presence clear with persistent loud calling, especially when breeding. Nests on the ground.

White-tailed Lapwing ■ *Vanellus leucurus* 28cm WS 75cm
(White-tailed Plover)

DESCRIPTION Large, fairly uniform plover. Uniform grey-brown above, head and breast; paler belly and vent. No black on head. Tail all white. Bill short and dark. Very long, bright yellow legs. In flight wings brown and black with white band above, black and white below. Much rarer **Sociable Lapwing** V. *gregarius* has dark on crown and lores, and in tail. **VOICE** Generally silent on passage. Alarm call *pee-wik*, often repeated. **DISTRIBUTION** In Egypt uncommon on passage in Nile Delta, Valley, and Fayoum; sometimes on coasts. Throughout Region scarce winter visitor from Central Asia and on passage, but also breeding resident along Gulf. Expanding. **HABITAT AND HABITS** Generally not in the open. Marshes, ponds, and ditches with dense vegetation and cover. Saline and freshwater habitats.

Northern Lapwing ■ *Vanellus vanellus* 30cm WS 70cm

DESCRIPTION Large plover. Dark above, glossed green/purple with pale fringes in winter. White below with orange-brown vent. Black and white on head with long, very thin crest often held erect. Short, straight bill. Legs orange-brown. In flight very broad, rounded wings, dark above with white below. Tail white with black subterminal band. **VOICE** Loud. Call in flight urgent *pee wich*, often repeated. Frequently calls at night. **DISTRIBUTION** In Egypt throughout Nile Delta and Valley and Fayoum, less often on coasts. Throughout Region common winter visitor and on passage. **HABITAT AND HABITS** Open country, agricultural land, pastures, and irrigated areas. Also marshes, riversides, and seashore. Often in flocks, sometimes large but also singly.

Red-wattled Lapwing ■ *Vanellus indicus* 34cm WS 80cm

DESCRIPTION Large lapwing. Pale brown above with white belly. Black crown to nape and back of neck and down central breast. Red eye-ring, lores, and bill-base. Long yellow legs. In flight wings very black and white; white tail with black subterminal band. **VOICE** Loud, urgent *cree cree …*, often accelerated with urgency. Penetrating. **DISTRIBUTION** Not in Egypt. In Region confined to Gulf south to Oman where can be common, for example in Muscat. **HABITAT AND HABITS** Loud bird that makes its presence known especially around breeding areas. Wetlands, pasture, and farmland, often close to water. Sociable.

Sanderling ■ *Calidris alba* 20cm WS 40cm

DESCRIPTION Slightly larger than Dunlin (p. 66). Non-breeding adult very pale – pale grey above with dark 'shoulder' patch and white below. Head pale with obscure white supercilium. Bill short, straight, and black. Legs black. In flight shows white wing-bar and black trailing edge, and white rump with dark central streak. In spring may have rufous and black scaling to upperparts.

VOICE Flight call short *plit*. **DISTRIBUTION** In Egypt in winter on Mediterranean coast. Also to Red Sea coasts on passage. In Region on passage to all coasts. In winter mainly on Arabian coasts. **HABITAT AND HABITS** Mainly coastal on sandy and muddy shorelines, beaches, and lagoons. Scarce inland. Very active, often in small flocks running along shoreline at edge of incoming surf.

Non-breeding

Little Stint ▪ *Calidris minuta* 14cm WS 29cm

DESCRIPTION Very small sandpiper – much smaller than Dunlin (p. 66). In winter fairly uniform grey above with some mottling. Rather plain head with whitish bill surround and obscure supercilium. White underparts with diffuse grey breast-band sometimes incomplete. In spring and autumn may show more rufous. Bill blackish, short, and straight. Legs blackish. In flight note short grey tail with white patches at base. **VOICE** High *stit* in flight. **DISTRIBUTION** In Egypt very common in winter and on passage in Delta, Valley, and along all coasts. In Region widespread throughout in winter and on passage. **HABITAT AND HABITS** Coasts, estuaries, and lagoons. Also inland on lakes, pools, reservoirs, and mudflats. Often in flocks on passage with other waders, where note size.

Temminck's Stint ▪ *Calidris temminckii* 14cm WS 29cm

DESCRIPTION Very similar to Little Stint (above) but longer tailed and with shorter, pale legs. Pale grey-brown above with rather plain face. White underparts with complete, clearly demarcated, grey-brown breast-band. At rest tail extends beyond primaries. Bill moderately long and slightly decurved. Legs pale yellowish. In erratic flight, when flushed, note longer, largely white tail. **VOICE** Trilling flight call rendered *trrrrr* … **DISTRIBUTION** In Egypt uncommon in winter and on passage in Delta, Valley, and along all coasts, but always much less common than Little. In Region on passage throughout and in winter in southern Arabia and Gulf. **HABITAT AND HABITS** Mostly inland on pools, lakes, and marshes, often staying close to vegetation. Also on muddy coasts. Retiring, creeping close to cover.

Curlew Sandpiper ▪ *Calidris ferruginea* 19cm WS 40cm

DESCRIPTION Similar to Dunlin (below) but longer legged and longer billed. Non-breeding adult plain grey above, white below, with grey streaking to breast-sides. Head has white supercilium. Bill blackish, longer than Dunlin's and more evenly curved down entire length, with fine tip. Legs dark grey. In flight shows narrow white wing-bar and clear white

rump. In spring may have much brick-red on underparts, neck, and head. **VOICE** In flight calls include *chureep*. **DISTRIBUTION** In Egypt scarce to fairly common on all coasts on passage. Some inland. In Region widespread throughout on passage. Winters on Arabian coasts, including Gulf. **HABITAT AND HABITS** Coastal, especially mudflats, estuaries, and lagoons. Also inland in marshes, wetlands, and lake shores. Less common than Dunlin, with which it often flocks.

Non-breeding

Dunlin ▪ *Calidris alpina* 18cm WS 38cm

DESCRIPTION Generally most common sandpiper in Region. Larger than stints. Non-breeding plain grey above with mottled grey breast and white belly. Head plain with obscure supercilium. Bill blackish, longer than stints' and slightly downcurved. Legs dark grey. In flight displays narrow white wing-bar and white rump with dark centre. Feet do

not project. In spring may have bright rufous upperparts and black belly. **VOICE** Clear *kreeep* in flight. **DISTRIBUTION** In Egypt very common winter visitor and on passage to all coasts, northern lakes, Delta, Fayoum, and Sinai. In Region widespread throughout in winter and on passage. **HABITAT AND HABITS** Coastal, especially in mudflats, estuaries, and lagoons. Also inland in marshes, wetlands, and lake shores. Often in flocks, sometimes large, especially on passage.

Broad-billed Sandpiper ▪ *Limicola falcinellus* 17cm WS 35cm

DESCRIPTION Like small, short-legged Dunlin (opposite). Streaked grey-brown above and white below, with heavily streaked breast. Head has somewhat snipe-like pattern, with striped crown and split pale supercilium. Bill rather long, straightish but with drooping tip. Legs yellow-grey. In winter more uniform grey above with dark feather shafts and more subdued head pattern. In flight quite dark, showing white rump with dark central stripe. **VOICE** Flight call dry, trilling *brreeep*. **DISTRIBUTION** In Egypt rare on passage to Mediterranean and Red Sea coasts, including Sinai and elsewhere, mainly in north. In Region on passage throughout. In winter on Arabian coasts. **HABITAT AND HABITS** In winter mainly on coasts. On passage also inland in marshes, wetlands, and lake margins.

Ruff ▪ *Philomachus pugnax* Male 28cm Female 22cm WS 56cm

DESCRIPTION Flamboyant breeding plumage not seen in Region. Variable. Male noticeably larger than female. Small headed and long necked. Mottled brown above, buffish on breast and with white belly. Male can be very white on head and neck. Bill medium in length, slightly downcurved, often dark and with whitish surround at base. Legs yellow to yellow-orange. In flight shows narrow white wing-bar and white patches at tail-base. **VOICE** Generally silent. **DISTRIBUTION** In Egypt flocks fairly common in Delta and Valley in winter. More widespread on passage. In Region in winter and on passage throughout. **HABITAT AND HABITS** Marshes, lake shores, pools, and wetlands. Also coasts and estuaries. Often appears shaggy in the field, with mantle ruffled. Any 'odd' looking wader should always be checked against Ruff.

Common Snipe ▪ *Gallinago gallinago* 27cm (including bill 7cm) WS 45cm

DESCRIPTION Cryptic, very long-billed wader. Upperparts complexly mottled black and brown with pale beige feather margins. Underparts with striped breast and closely barred flanks. Head has yellow-beige crown-stripe and supercilium, and dark crown and eye-stripe. Very long, straight bill. In flight note white trailing edges to wings and white belly.

Scarce **Jack Snipe** *Lymnocryptes minimus* much smaller, darker and with proportionately shorter bill. **VOICE** Loud *aartch* when flushed. **DISTRIBUTION** In Egypt common winter visitor to Delta, Valley, north Sinai, and Western Oases. More widespread on passage. In Region widespread throughout in winter and on passage. **HABITAT AND HABITS** Wetlands, marshes, water margins, and irrigation canals. Erupts when flushed, flying up in fast zigzags before settling.

Black-tailed Godwit ▪ *Limosa limosa* 40cm WS 74cm

DESCRIPTION Elegant, tall, very long-billed wader. Non-breeding adult largely plain, pale grey above including breast, neck, and head. White belly with some mottling. Short white supercilium and dark lores. Bill very long, straight, and largely pinkish with dark tip. Legs

long and dark grey. In flight shows square white rump with broad black tail-tip and clear white wing-bar. In spring begins showing much rufous above with dark barring. **VOICE** When agitated, loud *tikka tikka tikka*. **DISTRIBUTION** In Egypt fairly common on passage on northern lakes, Delta, Valley, and Mediterranean and Red Sea coasts; rarer in winter. In Region widespread throughout in winter and on passage. **HABITAT AND HABITS** Coastal mudflats, estuaries, and lagoons. Also inland on lake shores, marshes, and wetlands.

Bar-tailed Godwit ■ *Limosa lapponica* 38cm WS 72cm

DESCRIPTION Slightly smaller and shorter legged than Black-tailed Godwit (opposite). Non-breeding adult has grey upperparts streaked dark. Head and neck grey with crown streaked dark and long pale supercilium. Whitish below with some streaking on breast-sides. Bill somewhat shorter than Black-tailed's, slightly upcurved and dark with pink base. Longish, dark grey legs. In flight shows wedge-shaped white rump extending up back, no white wing-bar, and barred tail. In spring begins showing much rufous above, no barring. **VOICE** Call disyllabic *beb-beb* or *kwee kwee*. **DISTRIBUTION** In Egypt scarce on passage and in winter on coasts. In Region widespread throughout region, including Red Sea and Mediterranean coasts and Gulf. **HABITAT AND HABITS** Mainly coastal on muddy shorelines, beaches, and estuaries.

Whimbrel ■ *Numenius phaeopus* 41cm WS 83cm

DESCRIPTION Similar to Eurasian Curlew (p. 70) but smaller, darker, and with more strongly patterned head and shorter bill. Largely brown throughout, heavily mottled, streaked, and barred. Head has dark crown with paler central stripe and dark eye-stripe. Bill long and decurved but shorter than in most curlews, and curve less even, stronger towards tip. In flight shows white wedge extending up back from rump and barred tail. **VOICE** Call much more urgent than curlew's, rapid *bi bi bi bi bi* ... **DISTRIBUTION** In Egypt common on passage on all coasts and occasionally inland. A few overwinter. In Region widespread on passage throughout, with wintering birds on Arabian coasts. **HABITAT AND HABITS** On all coasts, reefs, and mangroves. Inland on lake shores, mudflats, and wetlands. Generally less common than Eurasian Curlew.

Eurasian Curlew ■ *Numenius arquata* 55cm WS 90cm
(Curlew)

DESCRIPTION Very large, long-billed wader. Largely brown, heavily mottled, streaked and barred. Head plain with at best obscure, pale supercilium and darker eye-stripe. Lower belly pale. Bill very long, slender, and evenly decurved; pinkish at base, and shorter in

male and juvenile than in female. Legs long and bluish-grey. In flight note white wedge on rump extending up back and barred tail. Race *orientalis* has pale underwing. **VOICE** Evocative, fluting *curl eee*. Shorter alarm *vi-vi-vuu*. **DISTRIBUTION** In Egypt uncommon winter visitor in Delta, North Coast, and northern lakes. Widespread on passage. In Region in winter and on passage throughout, especially on coasts. **HABITAT AND HABITS** On all coasts, reefs, and mangroves. Inland on large waterbodies, mudflats, and wetlands.

Common Redshank ■ *Tringa totanus* 27cm WS 58cm

DESCRIPTION Common, highly vocal wader. Heavily mottled, brown above and on head and neck to breast, with white eye-ring and diffuse supercilium not extending behind eye. Pale and subtly mottled below. Shortish bill dark with red base. Legs red. In flight note white wedge up back, barred tail with feet projecting, and bold white hindwing. **VOICE**

Vocal. Alarm piercing *keeyp keeyp keeyp* … Also more musical *djuu duu*. **DISTRIBUTION** In Egypt common in Delta, Valley, Western Oases, and on coasts in winter and on passage. Throughout Region on passage but in winter mainly in south. **HABITAT AND HABITS** Freshwater and saltwater bodies, including estuaries, mudflats, fresh and brackish marshes, lakes, and ponds. Singly or in small flocks. Call a familiar sound in suitable habitat.

Marsh Sandpiper ■ *Tringa stagnatilis* 23cm WS 57cm

DESCRIPTION Smaller, paler, more delicate version of Common Greenshank (below). Slim, uniform grey-brown above with much white on head and neck. Face white with white supercilium. Bill black, longish, needle-thin, and pointed. Legs yellowish-grey, very long, and thin. In flight dark above, with deep white wedge up back, white rump and white tail with diffuse barring. Legs extend well beyond tail. **VOICE** Like Common Greenshank's but higher pitched.
DISTRIBUTION Scarce in winter and on passage in Delta, Valley, Western Oases, and Red Sea coast. In Region widespread throughout on passage. Scarce in winter, mostly in south.
HABITAT AND HABITS Freshwater and coastal wetlands, including lakes, marshes, mudflats, and tidal creeks. Solitary or in small flocks.

Common Greenshank ■ *Tringa nebularia* 32cm WS 68cm

DESCRIPTION Like large, paler version of Common Redshank (opposite). Dark grey-brown above, paler especially on head, often appearing whitish, and streaked on neck and breast. Underparts white. Bill long, stout, and slightly upturned. Legs long and greyish-green. In flight shows dark wings (with no white), contrasting with white back and rump, and largely white tail with obscure barring. **VOICE** Loud, three-syllable *tyuw tyuw tyuw* and single-note *kyu* alarm. **DISTRIBUTION** In Egypt in winter mainly in Delta; more widespread on passage. In Region widespread on passage throughout, with some in winter, especially in south Arabia and Oman.
HABITAT AND HABITS Freshwater and saltwater bodies, including estuaries, mudflats, fresh and brackish marshes, lakes, and ponds. Singly or in small flocks. Active feeder, running after prey in shallows.

Green Sandpiper ■ *Tringa ochropus* 23cm WS 58cm

DESCRIPTION Dark sandpiper, slightly smaller than Common Redshank (p. 70). Upperparts predominantly dark blackish grey-green, very finely speckled. Dark breast clearly demarcated from white underparts. Head has faint pale supercilium barely extending behind eye. Bill moderately long and straight. Legs grey-green. In flight note

all-dark wings, white rump and white tail with broad black bands, and legs barely projecting. **VOICE** Clear whistle when flushed, *kleweeed wit wit*. When alarmed urgent *tlip tlip tlip*. **DISTRIBUTION** In Egypt scarce in winter in Delta and Valley; locally elsewhere. Widespread on passage. In Region on passage and in winter throughout. **HABITAT AND HABITS** Water margins, generally with cover, such as lakes, rivers, ponds, canal banks, marshes, and even mangroves. Compared with Wood Sandpiper (below) note darker upperparts and broad bands on white tail.

Wood Sandpiper ■ *Tringa glareola* 20cm WS 56cm

DISTRIBUTION Smaller and more patterned than Green Sandpiper (above). Upperparts strongly mottled brown and buff. Breast diffusely streaked brown, merging into pale underparts (clear demarcation in Green). Head has prominent pale supercilium extending behind eye, and dark eye-stripe and lores. Bill moderately long and straight. Legs yellowish-green. In flight mottled brown above, with white rump and tail with narrow banding, and legs extending well beyond tail-tip. **VOICE** Loud, multi-syllable *tchiff iff iff* … and clipped *gip gip* … **DISTRIBUTION** In Egypt scarce winter visitor to Delta and

Valley, but also elsewhere. Widespread and most common on passage. In Region throughout on passage; rarer in winter, largely in south Arabia. **HABITAT AND HABITS** Freshwater, brackish and coastal marshes and mudflats, lakes, and small pools. Singly or in small flocks. Bobs like Common Sandpiper (opposite) but less exaggerated.

Terek Sandpiper ■ *Xenus cinereus* 24cm WS 58cm

DESCRIPTION Highly distinctive, long necked, short-legged sandpiper. Upperparts uniform, rather pale, grey. Breast greyish with white underparts. Head grey with slight pale supercilium, darker lores, and noticeably steep forehead. Bill long, upturned, and dark, with dull yellow-orange base. Legs yellow to orange. In flight note all-grey tail and rump, and narrow white trailing edge to secondaries. **VOICE** Short, multi-syllabic whistle, *twit twit* … **DISTRIBUTION**
In Egypt generally rare on passage to Sinai and Red Sea coasts. In Region on passage and in winter to Red Sea, south Arabian and Gulf coasts. Much rarer on passage in Mediterranean. **HABITAT AND HABITS** Largely coastal on reefs, mudflats, saltmarshes, and mangroves. Occasionally inland on passage. Active feeder, scurrying forwards with head lowered, lunging at prey.

Common Sandpiper ■ *Actitis hypoleucos* 19cm WS 38cm

DESCRIPTION Long-bodied, short-necked, short-tailed sandpiper that constantly bobs rear body up and down. Upperparts uniform grey-brown. Brown breast sharply demarcated from white underparts, with white extending around breast-sides. Head has dark eye-stripe and lores, and obscure white supercilium. Tail extends beyond wing-tips. Bill shortish and straight. Legs dull greenish. In flight shows dark rump and bold white wing-bar. **VOICE** Descending high-pitched whistling in flight. Loud *heeep* when alarmed. **DISTRIBUTION**
In Egypt widespread and common on passage; scarcer in winter in Delta, Valley, Western Oases, and coasts. **HABITAT AND HABITS** Mostly freshwater bodies, including rivers, lakes, canal banks, and open marshland. Also coasts. Generally singly. Exaggerated bobbing highly distinctive even at distance. Flies low over the water with rapid, active flight punctuated by short glides on stiff, downcurved wings.

Ruddy Turnstone ■ *Arenaria interpres* 23cm WS 52cm

DESCRIPTION Distinctive stocky wader. In summer has chestnut and black upperparts and striking pied head and breast. In winter mottled black-brown above, including most of head and breast, with blackish breast-band standing out. White below. Bill short,

pointed, and slightly upturned. Legs short and orange. In flight very pied – white on back, rump, tail, and wing-bar. **VOICE** In flight low *chk* and *krt krt krt krt …* **DISTRIBUTION** In Egypt scarce on passage and in winter along all coasts. Few inland. In Region on Mediterranean coast and all Arabian coasts including Gulf on passage and in winter. Rare inland. **HABITAT AND HABITS** Rocky and sandy coasts and lake shores. Small flocks and singles work shoreline, picking at pebbles and weeds in search of prey.

Red-necked Phalarope ■ *Phalaropus lobatus* 18cm WS 36cm

DESCRIPTION Tiny, active wader. In summer largely dark grey-blue with broad chestnut breast and collar, and white throat. Non-breeding pale grey above with white head, pale grey crown, and bold black mask through and behind eye. Black on hindcrown. Bill black, slender, and needle-like. Often seen swimming, sitting high on the water with pointed rear end. **VOICE** Short *krit* when alarmed. **DISTRIBUTION** In Egypt rare on passage, especially in north, Sinai, and Red Sea coast. In Region widespread throughout on passage.

Pelagic in winter, including Arabian Sea. **HABITAT AND HABITS** Mainly coastal on passage but also lakes and ponds. Characteristic swimming action, spinning in tight circles to stir up food. Also around large birds such as flamingos, picking up items they stir up.

Arctic Skua ■ *Stercorarius parasiticus* 47cm (including tail streamers 7cm) WS 114cm

DESCRIPTION Like small dark gull. Uniform dark brown upperparts. Dark brown tail with pointed streamers. Some birds all dark. Pale-phase birds have whitish underparts, throat, and neck, latter with yellow tinge. Dark cap and pale bill surround. Bill rather slender. In flight note pointed dark wings with pale patch at bases of primaries. Very similar **Pomarine Skua** *S. pomarinus* has deeper chest, heavier bill, and blunt streamers. **VOICE** Alarm rendered *pjew*. **DISTRIBUTION** In Egypt both species scarce visitors on passage off Mediterranean and Red Sea coasts. In Region on passage in Red Sea and Gulf; on passage and in winter in Arabian Sea. **HABITAT AND HABITS** Pelagic and coastal. Piratic harassing and attacking of birds up to gull size in flight.

Sooty Gull ■ *Larus hemprichii* 44cm WS 112cm

DESCRIPTION Brown, heavy-billed gull, slightly larger than White-eyed Gull (p. 76). Adult has dark brown upperparts; pale below with brownish chest. Head dark brown with white collar and small white patch above eye (above and below in White-eyed). Yellow bill heavy, with red and dark tip. Legs yellowish. Immatures paler and more scalloped above. In flight dark underwing. Differs from White-eyed by no white below eye, color of heavy bill, and brown upperparts. **VOICE** Harsh *krraaar*. **DISTRIBUTION** In Egypt throughout Red Sea, breeding from Hurghada south and in Gulf of Aqaba. In Region along entire Red Sea coast of Arabia, south Arabia, and southern Gulf. Disperses rarely to northern Gulf. **HABITAT AND HABITS** Coastal, including in ports and harbors. Breeds on cliffs and offshore islands.

White-eyed Gull ■ *Larus leucophthalmus* 41cm WS 107cm

DESCRIPTION Black-headed, long-billed gull. Adult has grey upperparts with black primaries; white below with greyish on chest. Head black, extending down throat, with distinct white patch above and below eye. Bill long and slender, with dark red base. Legs yellow. Immatures duller and browner. In flight shows dark underwing. Compared with Sooty Gull (p. 75) note white above and below eye, color of slender bill, and less brown above. **VOICE** As Sooty's but less harsh. **DISTRIBUTION** Red Sea near endemic. In Egypt throughout Red Sea, breeding from Hurghada south and in Gulf of Aqaba. In Region entire Red Sea coast of Arabia, dispersing south as far as Gulf of Oman. **HABITAT AND HABITS** Coastal, including in ports and harbors. Breeds on cliffs and offshore islands.

Black-headed Gull ▪ *Chroicocephalus ridibundus* 38cm WS 93cm

DESCRIPTION Generally most common smaller gull. Adult summer grey above, white below, with chocolate-brown hood, not extending on to nape, with incomplete white eye-ring. In winter head white, strongly smudged dark behind and above eye. Bill small, slender, and dark red; paler in winter. Iris dark. Legs reddish. In flight note white leading edge to wing and black tips to primaries. More local **Mediterranean Gull** *Larus melanocephalus* has black head and no black in wings. **VOICE** Loud *krreeearrr* and short *kek*. **DISTRIBUTION** In Egypt very common on passage and in winter. In Region common in winter and on passage throughout.

HABITAT AND HABITS Coastal and on lagoons and lakes, fresh and brackish, and on rivers. Also ports, harbors, and inland, including on rubbish tips.

Black-headed Gull   Mediterranean Gull

Slender-billed Gull ▪ *Chroicocephalus genei* 42cm WS 98cm

DESCRIPTION Pale, long-necked, long-billed gull. Larger and longer billed than winter Black-headed Gull (above). All white (including head in summer) with pale grey mantle. In summer often rose tinged below. In winter has faint dark ear-spot. Bill dark red and long. Iris pale. Legs dull red, paler in winter. Immature has paler bare parts. In flight white leading edge to wing and black tips to primaries. **VOICE** Rather low *yaarrrr*. **DISTRIBUTION** In Egypt very local resident breeder, for example in Fayoum. Much more widespread in winter and on passage. In Region widespread throughout in winter and on passage. Breeds in northernmost Gulf. **HABITAT AND HABITS** Mainly coastal, especially in winter, but also on large inland waters, lakes, fresh and brackish, and rivers. Colonial breeder.

Audouin's Gull ■ *Larus audouinii* 49cm WS 124cm

DESCRIPTION Mediterranean endemic. Adult smaller than Yellow-legged Gull (opposite) with grey upperparts, white underparts tinged grey in summer, and all-white head. Bill rather short, and dark red with yellow tip. Iris dark. Legs green-grey, appearing

blackish. In flight elegant, pale grey above, with black wing-tips with very small white spots on primaries. **VOICE** Loud, coarse *aarrgh*. **DISTRIBUTION** In Egypt fairly rare on passage to Mediterranean coast including north Sinai. In Region uncommon winter visitor to eastern Mediterranean. **HABITAT AND HABITS** Coastal nesting on Mediterranean cliffs and islands. Formerly very rare but although still uncommon has increased in numbers in recent decades. Note leg and bill color and slightly smaller size than similar species like Yellow-legged.

Lesser Black-backed Gull ■ *Larus fuscus* 53cm WS 127cm

DESCRIPTION Race in Region **Baltic Gull** *L. f. fuscus*. White-headed gull with very dark mantle. Adult has blackish mantle and wings. Underparts white. Head white with sparse streaking in winter and pale iris. Bill yellow with small red mandibular spot. Legs yellow. In flight shows very little white on primaries. Much larger **Heuglin's Gull** *L. f. heuglini* has greyer mantle and dark iris; winters in south Arabia and Gulf. **VOICE** Deep, nasal *kyow*. **DISTRIBUTION** In Egypt winter visitor and on passage along North Coast to Delta and Sinai and Red Sea coast. Also Delta and Valley. In Region along Mediterranean Levant and on all Arabian coasts including Gulf. **HABITAT AND HABITS** Mainly coastal. Less often inland on large lakes.

Baltic Gull   *Heuglin's Gull*

Yellow-legged Gull ▪ *Larus michahellis* 52–58cm WS 130cm

DESCRIPTION Large, white-headed gull. Breeding adult has pale grey mantle with black primaries showing clear white spots. Underparts white. Head has little or no streaking in winter. Eyes have pale irises. Yellow bill heavy, with large red spot on lower mandible and strongly curved tip. Legs bright yellow. Scarcer **Armenian Gull** *L. armenicus* has darker mantle, dark iris, and black band on bill. **VOICE** Deep, nasal *kyow*. **DISTRIBUTION** In Egypt breeds on western Mediterranean coast, and winter visitor along North Coast and Sinai. Armenian also south to Delta and Red Sea coasts. In Region resident along Mediterranean coast, with winter dispersal; Armenian as far as Gulf. **HABITAT AND HABITS** Mostly coastal but also on large inland waters. Often seen around ports and harbors. Appears to be expanding its range.

Yellow-legged Gull

Armenian Gull

Gull-billed Tern ▪ *Gelochelidon nilotica* 40cm WS 95cm

DESCRIPTION Similar to Sandwich Tern (p. 81). In summer grey upperparts (darker than Sandwich's) extend to rump and tail. White underparts. Black cap with no crest. Tail slightly forked. Bill shortish, thick, and all black. Legs black. In winter crown white with dark around eye and ear-coverts. In flight shows dark trailing edges to primaries. **VOICE** Calls include *ker-wick*. **DISTRIBUTION** In Egypt on passage and in winter on North Coast, Delta, along Nile, and also Red Sea. In Region local summer breeder in Levant, resident in northern Gulf and on passage throughout. **HABITAT AND HABITS** Coastal, especially on sandy shores. Also on large lakes and rivers, marshland, and associated pasture. Feeds on fish but also hawks for large insects.

Caspian Tern ■ *Hydroprogne caspia* 52cm WS 133cm

DESCRIPTION Huge tern. Adult summer very large; pale grey above and white below. Crown black with short, angular crest. Tail relatively short with shallow fork. Bill massive; bright red with dark tip. Legs dark. In winter white streaking on forehead. In flight shows extensive dark shading to undersides of wing-tips. **VOICE** Very vocal, especially when

breeding. Most commonly very loud *kraaarrkk*. **DISTRIBUTION** In Egypt localized breeder along Red Sea coast. On passage along Mediterranean and Red Sea. In Region local resident along Red Sea and Gulf coasts, and on passage throughout. Winters off Arabia. **HABITAT AND HABITS** Breeds on offshore islands. Otherwise largely sandy and rocky coasts, lagoons, and estuaries, but also large inland freshwater bodies and marshes.

Greater Crested Tern ■ *Sterna bergii* 46cm WS 105cm
(Swift Tern, Crested Tern)

DESCRIPTION Only slightly smaller than Caspian Tern (above). In summer a large, slim tern, grey above (darker than Lesser Crested Tern, opposite) and white below. Black cap with rather shaggy crest. Bill long, slightly drooping, and lemon-yellow, separated from black cap by white. Tail moderately forked. Legs black. In winter black confined to nape. **VOICE** Fairly deep *kree-rit* or *kraarrkk*. **DISTRIBUTION** In Egypt uncommon along Red Sea coast, where breeds. In Region summer breeder in Red Sea, along southern

Arabia and Gulf, with dispersal through these areas on passage and in winter. **HABITAT AND HABITS** Generally breeds on offshore islands. Coastal on sandy and rocky shores. Often with other terns (including more numerous Lesser Crested), where comparative size and bill shape and color important.

Lesser Crested Tern ▪ *Sterna bengalensis* 40cm WS 92cm

DESCRIPTION Smaller than similar Greater Crested Tern (opposite). Adult summer pale grey above and white below. Black cap unseparated from bill (white gap in Greater Crested), with crest on nape. Bill slender, pointed, and pale orange. Tail moderately forked. Legs dark. In winter bill paler and often with much white on forehead. **VOICE** Coarse *kerrickk*. **DISTRIBUTION** In Egypt migrant breeder along Red Sea coast; rare straggler to Mediterranean. In Region summer breeder along Red Sea coasts and Gulf, with dispersal through these areas and Arabian Sea on passage and in winter. **HABITAT AND HABITS** Generally breeds on offshore islands. Coastal on sandy and rocky shores. Often with other terns, where comparative size, bill shape, and color important. Usually more numerous than Greater Crested.

Sandwich Tern ▪ *Sterna sandvicensis* 41cm (including tail streamers 6cm) WS 93cm

DESCRIPTION Gull-sized tern but much slimmer. Summer adult has pale grey upperparts and white underparts. Black cap with angular, shaggy crest. Tail white and deeply forked. Black bill long, straight, and slender, with yellow tip. Legs black. In winter has white on forehead. Powerful flight, showing darker outer primaries. **VOICE** Vocal around colonies, with loud *kerr-rick*. **DISTRIBUTION** Along Egypt's Mediterranean coast in winter. More widespread on passage, including Red Sea. In Region very local summer breeder in northern Gulf. In winter around all Arabian coasts, Gulf, and Mediterranean. **HABITAT AND HABITS** Coastal, in Egypt including northern coastal lakes. Flight buoyant; head often held at an angle with bill pointing sharply down.

Common Tern ■ *Sterna hirundo* 38cm (including tail streamers 7cm) WS 75cm

DESCRIPTION In summer grey upperparts and pale grey below (much paler than in White-cheeked Tern, below, and with no contrasting white cheek). White tail streamers. Long, pale reddish bill with dark tip. Legs red. Differs from White-cheeked by bill color and slightly longer legs. In winter white below with white forehead and dark bill. In flight shows diffuse darker wedge on primaries. **VOICE** Hard *kit* and longer *kreee-aar*. **DISTRIBUTION** In Egypt fairly common on passage on Mediterranean and Red Sea

coasts. More occasional inland. In Region very local summer breeder in Mediterranean Levant. On passage throughout. Winters in south Arabia. **HABITAT AND HABITS** Coastal and maritime breeding on beaches and offshore islands. Also on larger inland waters, rivers, and lakes on passage.

White-cheeked Tern ■ *Sterna repressa* 36cm (including tail streamers 6cm) WS 61cm

DESCRIPTION Like Common Tern (above) but slightly smaller. Adult summer dark grey above; all grey below with white cheek-stripe. Crown black. Tail has long streamers. Bill dark red and slender. Legs dark red. In winter white below and on forehead, with dark

bill. In flight shows pale centre to underwing. From summer differs from Whiskered Tern (p. 84) also by larger size and long tail streamers. **VOICE** Like Common Tern's – hard *kit* and longer *kreee-aar*. **DISTRIBUTION** Summer breeder in Egyptian Red Sea, with winter dispersal to Gulfs of Suez and Aqaba. In Region breeds throughout Arabian Red Sea and from Oman north through Gulf. On passage throughout; less common in winter. **HABITAT AND HABITS** Breeds on offshore islands. Otherwise coastal and maritime.

Bridled Tern ■ *Onychoprion anaethetus* 39cm (including tail streamers 8cm) WS 70cm

DESCRIPTION Dark, slender tern. Blackish upperparts with dark grey-brown mantle. Black crown, nape, and through eye. White forehead extends behind eye, ending in point; white throat and underparts. Tail deeply forked, with long streamers. Bill dark and slender. Legs dark. Larger **Sooty Tern** *O. fuscata* has shorter tail streamers; blacker above with white not extending behind eye and ending bluntly. **VOICE** Variety of calls, including various *kaarrrs*. **DISTRIBUTION** Summer breeder in Egyptian Red Sea. In Region breeds throughout Red Sea, along southern Arabian coast to Gulf. Throughout on passage. Winters in Arabian Sea. Sooty breeds off Oman and winters farther east. **HABITATS AND HABITS** Breeds on offshore islands, for example mouth of Gulf of Aqaba. Maritime in winter.

Little Tern ■ *Sternula albifrons* 23cm WS 50cm

DESCRIPTION 'Marsh tern' in size. Tiny – in summer note pale grey above and white below. Black cap extends down back of neck. Black lores and white forehead extend in point beyond eye. Tail moderately forked. Bill yellow with black tip. Legs orange-yellow. In winter black bill; more white on crown. Very similar **Saunder's Little Tern** *S. saundersi* has white forehead with blunt end before eye. **VOICE** Agitated, hoarse *kree-it*. **DISTRIBUTION** In Egypt breeds along North Coast and Delta to Fayoum. More widespread in winter, including Red Sea. In Region, Mediterranean, Levant, and locally Gulf. Some dispersal in winter. Saunder's breeds on Arabian coasts – recently southern Egypt. **HABITAT AND HABITS** Coastal and inland, breeding on sandy beaches. Saunder's more strictly coastal.

Juvenile

Whiskered Tern ■ *Chlidonias hybrida* 26cm WS 72cm

DESCRIPTION Like White-cheeked Tern (p. 82) but lacks tail streamers. In summer dark grey throughout, in flight showing more silver-grey on wings, rump, and tail. Crown down back of neck black with bright white cheeks. Bill dark red. Legs red. In winter

pale grey above and white below, with white forehead, dark behind ear continuous with crown, and no dark patch at breast-sides. **VOICE** Squeaky cries and harsher *chrkk*. **DISTRIBUTION** In Egypt widespread on passage through Delta and Valley to Western Oases and Sinai, and along coasts. Also in winter. In Region on passage throughout, with some in winter, generally in south. **HABITAT AND HABITS** Usually on inland lakes, rivers, ponds, and marshes, but also coastal on passage and in winter.

White-winged Black Tern ■ *Chlidonias leucopterus* 22cm WS 65cm

DESCRIPTION Striking black and white 'marsh tern'. In summer black head, breast, and belly. Dark grey mantle. White wing-coverts, lower belly, rump, and tail. Bill black. Legs red. In winter upperparts pale grey; white below and on rump. Head white, streaked on crown with dark ear-spot not connected to cap. Larger **Black Tern** C. *niger* all black and grey in summer, with black legs. In winter has dark patch at breast-sides. **VOICE** Calls include harsh *chrre* and softer *kek*. **DISTRIBUTION** In Egypt widespread on passage through Delta and Valley and along coasts. Black scarcer. In Region on passage throughout. Local breeder in Gulf. Scarce in winter. **HABITAT AND HABITS** Breeds on inland wetlands. On passage on lakes, rivers, and marshes, but also coastal.

African Skimmer ■ *Rhynchops flavirostris* 38cm WS 106cm

DESCRIPTION Very distinctive, tern-like waterbird. Breeding adult has all-black back, mantle and wings. Underparts white. Head white with black hood, nape, and down back of neck. In winter has diffuse white collar. Bill bright orange-red with lower mandible longer than upper and yellow tipped. Red legs very short. Graceful in flight, showing white trailing edge to secondaries. **VOICE** Rather high-pitched wittering. **DISTRIBUTION** In Egypt probably breeds in south on sandbanks in Lake Nasser. Vagrant to south Arabia.

HABITAT AND HABITS Generally inland on large lakes and rivers. Gregarious, nesting in colonies. Feeds flying low over the water with long lower mandible cutting the water, snapping up fish on contact.

Lichtenstein's Sandgrouse ■ *Pterocles lichtensteinii* 25cm WS 50cm

DESCRIPTION Small, short-tailed sandgrouse. Male compact, buffish; heavily but finely barred black and white throughout. Plain orange on breast bordered black above and below. Head has white above and behind eye, with two vertical black bands. Bill pinkish. Female sandy-buff, finely banded throughout, and lacks male's head pattern. Tail short. In flight dark brown primaries.

VOICE Calls musical *wee-ak* and harsher *ahrrk*.

DISTRIBUTION In Egypt locally common resident in southern Eastern Desert and south Sinai. In Region from Naqab down western Arabia, south Arabia to Oman, and north to southern Gulf.

HABITATS AND HABITS Mountains, but also down to sea level, rocky deserts, and rocky wadi floors. In singles or small flocks; often crepuscular or active at night. Generally drinks after sunset.

Crowned Sandgrouse ■ *Pterocles coronatus* 28cm WS 57cm

DESCRIPTION Pale, short-tailed sandgrouse. Note head pattern. Male sandy throughout, blotched pale on wings and with yellow on head and neck. Pale below. Blue-grey from behind eye and black on forehead and bill-base. *P. c. saturatus* in Oman darker. Female

finely barred throughout, with yellow throat and neck. Short tailed. In flight shows black secondaries and primaries. Similar but larger **Black-bellied Sandgrouse** *P. orientalis* has black belly; may breed in Naqab. **VOICE** Flight call harsh *kah-kata-kata kat-ah*. **DISTRIBUTION** In Egypt local resident southwest of Delta, Eastern Desert, and Sinai. In Region resident in Naqab and much of Oman. Very local elsewhere in Arabia. **HABITAT AND HABITS** Rocky deserts, semi-deserts, and dry plains with sparse vegetation. In flocks at water sources in mornings.

Spotted Sandgrouse ■ *Pterocles senegallus* 36cm
(including 5cm tail projection) WS 59cm

DESCRIPTION Pale sandgrouse with long tail projections. Male overall sandy-orange and grey-banded on wings. Head, neck, and breast dove-grey, with orange throat and cheeks. Pale belly, darker rump. Tail has long, pointed central feathers. Female pale sandy throughout, with speckled upperparts and breast. Orange throat and cheeks. In flight note black secondaries. **Chestnut-bellied Sandgrouse** *P. exustus* similar, but with no grey and dark brown belly, recently rediscovered in Egypt. **VOICE** Call *kwitt-o* in flight.

DISTRIBUTION In Egypt only sandgrouse resident in much of Western Desert. Also Eastern Desert and Sinai. In Region local resident in Levant, eastern Arabia, and Oman. Chestnut-bellied local in southern and eastern Arabia. **HABITAT AND HABITS** Sandy deserts and semi-deserts. In flocks at water sources in mornings.

Rock Dove ▪ *Columba livia* 33cm WS 65cm
(Feral Pigeon)

DESCRIPTION Wild ancestor of familiar domestic pigeon. Wild birds dark grey above glossed green and purple on neck. Underparts, wings, and mantle pale grey. Two broad black wing-bars. Back white. Rump and tail grey with black terminal band. Dark bill with pale cere. Red legs. Feral and domestic birds vary; some as wild type, to all dark, piebald, reddish, and white. **VOICE** Familiar, repeated *druuuooo oo*. **DISTRIBUTION** In Egypt wild birds resident along Delta and Valley margins, Eastern Desert, Sinai and Western Oases. In Region wild birds resident throughout, except northern and central Arabia. Feral/domestic birds around human habitation everywhere. **HABITAT AND HABITS** Wild birds resident in mountainous desert and semi-desert country. Also sea cliffs. Feral/domestic birds in farmland, cities, towns, and villages.

Eurasian Collared Dove ▪
Streptopelia decaocto 32cm WS 51cm
(Collared Dove)

DESCRIPTION Fairly large, all-pale dove. Pale buff-grey throughout with off-white panel on wing and darker primaries. Pale head, neck, and underparts with incomplete black collar at back of neck. Longish tail pale above and with much white below, contrasting with undertail-coverts, especially noticeable in flight. Legs reddish. **VOICE** Three syllables rendered *doo-dooooooo-doo*. **DISTRIBUTION** In Egypt resident in Delta, Valley, Suez Canal, and north Sinai. In Region resident in Levant, much of Arabia, and throughout Gulf. Range expanding in many areas. **HABITAT AND HABITS** Agricultural areas, gardens, parks in cities, and towns and villages. Similar **African Collared Dove** *S. risoria* (more contrasting tail pattern, darker flight feathers, and white undertail-coverts) in southeastern Egypt and eastern Arabia, in drier, semi-desert habitats.

Eurasian Collared Dove

African Collared Dove

European Turtle Dove ■ *Streptopelia turtur* 27cm WS 47cm
(Turtle Dove)

DESCRIPTION Quite dark dove, though race *arenicola* in Arabia is paler. Upperparts tortoiseshell with dark brown feathers margined with orange. Pale grey head and grey-pink face and breast, whitish below. Striped black and white patch on sides of neck. Eye has pale iris and red orbital ring. Legs red. In flight note grey rump and tail strongly patterned black and white. **VOICE** Purring *turrrr turrrr turrrr*, often repeated. **DISTRIBUTION** In

Egypt fairly common summer visitor to Delta, Valley, north Sinai, and Western Oases. Widespread on passage. In Region summer breeder in Levant and patchily through Arabia and Gulf. On passage throughout. **HABITAT AND HABITS** Open woodland, oases, gardens, and farmland. Generally not a bird of towns and villages. Declining everywhere.

Laughing Dove ■ *Streptopelia senegalensis* 25cm WS 43cm
(Palm Dove)

DESCRIPTION Small, slim dove. Upperparts reddish-brown with pale blue-grey wing-panel. Head, neck, and breast grey-mauve with finely speckled black gorget. Whitish below with all-white undertail-coverts. Tail dark grey above. In flight note dark wing-tips, bluish panel on secondaries, and white corners to dark tail. **VOICE** Six-syllable call. *Doo doo doo doo doo doo.* **DISTRIBUTION** In Egypt very common resident throughout Delta and

Valley, along North and Red Sea coasts, Sinai, and Western Oases. In Region throughout Levant south through Naqab and Arabia, except centre, and Gulf. **HABITAT AND HABITS** Farmland, orchards, oases, cities, towns, and villages. Very familiar even in large urban centres such as Cairo and Alexandria.

Namaqua Dove ■ *Oena capensis* 25cm (including tail 11cm) WS 31cm

DESCRIPTION Tiny, long-tailed dove – like a large Budgerigar. Male pale buff-grey throughout with black spots on wings and dark primaries. Face, throat, and upper breast black. Pale below. Tail very long, slender, and black with white tips. Bill red with yellow tip. Female paler, lacking black on head and neck. In flight note rufous wings. Juvenile scaled and scalloped. **VOICE**
Low, extended *coo*. Not vocal.
DISTRIBUTION In Egypt confined to southeast, where records are increasing. In Region resident in Naqab and patchily across much of Arabia and Gulf. Some dispersal, and range expanding. **HABITAT AND HABITS** Open country, semi-deserts, acacia and thorn scrub, and wadi floors. Very distinctive but quietly unobtrusive. Generally feeds on the ground.

Female

Rose-ringed Parakeet ■ *Psittacula krameri* 40cm

DESCRIPTION Loud green parrot. Bright green throughout, including very long, slender, pointed tail. Male has black throat and narrow black collar with rose-pink to nape. Female lacks collar. Bill has bright red upper mandible and red orbital ring. In fast, direct flight, note pointed wings with darker flight feathers. Much more localized introduction, **Alexandrine Parakeet** *P. eupatria*, is almost twice the size, with much larger and heavier bill, and maroon 'shoulders'. **VOICE** Very loud and vocal, with loud, piercing screams. **DISTRIBUTION** In Egypt introduced/escaped, with established populations in many districts of Cairo, Alexandria, and elsewhere. In Region established in parts of Levant, eastern Arabia, and Gulf. **HABITAT AND HABITS** Established in areas around human habitation, including large cities, parks, and gardens.

Common Cuckoo ■ *Cuculus canorus* 34cm WS 57cm

DESCRIPTION Superficially hawk-like. Male blue-grey above, including head and breast; darker on wings. Underparts pale with regular dark barring. Slim bill, dark with yellow base. Yellow eye-ring. Tail long and graduated. Female similar or entirely rufous-brown; paler below and barred black throughout. Juvenile as female rufous form, but darker with white patch on nape. **VOICE** Song onomatopoeic *kuk-koo*. Female has bubbling call. **DISTRIBUTION** In Egypt scarce on passage, especially North Coast including Sinai, Delta, and Valley. In Region local breeder in Levant. Widespread on passage throughout. **HABITAT AND HABITS** Breeds in open woodland, farmland, groves, and plantations. On passage also coastal scrubland. Hawk-like, but note pointed wings and long, graduated tail. Often perches with tail raised and wings dropped.

Senegal Coucal ■ *Centropus senegalensis* 40cm

DESCRIPTION Large and long tailed. Upperparts bright chestnut with long, all-dark tail with rounded end. Head and nape black down to dark brown mantle. Underparts creamy-white. Iris red. Bill dark and heavy. Juvenile has dark barring on upperparts. In flight note long tail and rounded wings. **VOICE** Sonorous *hoo hoo hoo hu hu hu ...* accelerating and tailing off like 'blowing over a bottle top'. **DISTRIBUTION** Egypt only. Resident in Delta, Valley, and Fayoum. **HABITAT AND HABITS** Farmland, often near water, dense vegetation along irrigation canals, thickets, gardens, and plantations. Very distinctive jizz – rather clumsy, crashing through trees or foraging on the ground. Lumbering, flapping flight interspersed with glides. Not often seen, but voice characteristic of Egyptian countryside.

Barn Owl ■ *Tyto alba* 33–39cm WS 80–95cm

DESCRIPTION Medium-sized, very pale owl.
Sandy-gold above, mottled greyish on wings
and crown. Pure white below, sometimes tinged
ochre. Heart-shaped face white with dark eyes.
In flight all pale below with blunt wings, like
an enormous moth. **VOICE** Rattled shriek or
squeal. Young utter incessant, noisy hiss at
nest. **DISTRIBUTION** In Egypt widespread
resident. Can be common along North Coast,
Delta, Valley, and Sinai. In Region resident
throughout, although absent from desert areas
with dispersal in winter. **HABITAT AND
HABITS** Open country, acacia and palm
groves, farmland, orchards, towns and villages,
and even cities. Nocturnal. At night very pale
below. In Cairo can be confused with flying
Senegal Thick-knee (p. 56) from below at
night, but note broad, rounded wings.

Pharaoh Eagle Owl ■ *Bubo ascalaphus* 38–50cm WS 115–130cm

DESCRIPTION Large eared owl.
Upperparts sandy, barred, and mottled
with dark and pale. Underparts pale buff,
streaked dark on breast, and mottled rufous
below. Facial disk pale buff with narrow
black margin. Short, black-lined ear-
tufts. Eyes orange-yellow. Now separated
from much larger, darker **Eurasian Eagle
Owl** *B. bubo*, a local resident in Levant.
VOICE Song loud, sonorous booming.
Call trisyllabic *hoo oo-oo* with emphasis
on first note. **DISTRIBUTION** In Egypt
local resident over much of Eastern and
Western Deserts, Valley, Delta margins,
and Sinai. In Region patchily resident
from southern Levant south through
much of Arabia and Gulf. **HABITAT
AND HABITS** Rocky and sandy deserts,
wadis, crags and ravines, desert margins,
and ruins including archaeological sites.
Largely nocturnal.

Hume's Owl ▪ *Strix butleri* 32cm WS 75cm

(Hume's Tawny Owl)

DESCRIPTION Medium-sized, thickset desert owl. Rather plain; pale grey-buff above and pale sandy-gold below, subtly mottled. Large headed with pale facial disk with narrow dark margin, darker wedge down centre of forehead, and whitish 'eyebrows'. Eyes orange-yellow. In flight wings and tail strongly barred. Differs from larger Pharaoh Eagle Owl (p. 91) by size, unstreaked underparts, and lack of ear-tufts. **VOICE** Far-carrying *hooo hoo-hoo hoo-hoo*. **DISTRIBUTION** Endemic to Region. In Egypt very local breeder in south Sinai and Eastern Desert. In Region very scarce breeder, patchily distributed from Naqab south through Arabia. **HABITAT AND HABITS** Desert owl. Found in desert mountains, cliffs, wadis, and ravines. Nocturnal. Preys largely on desert rodents.

Little Owl ■ *Athene noctua* 24cm WS 55cm

DESCRIPTION Small, compact, large-headed owl. Brown above, boldly spotted with white. Underparts white, streaked brown. Head and neck more finely spotted. Head flat topped; face framed white, with large yellow eyes. Legs long and white. In flight brown, spotted with white above. **VOICE** Short *kee kee kee* when alarmed. Also more drawn-out *kee eww*. **DISTRIBUTION** In Egypt widespread resident. Can be common throughout North Coast, Delta, and Valley to Western Oases and Sinai. In Region widespread resident breeder. Very pale race *lilith*, sometimes considered separate species, in Arabia and elsewhere, including Sinai. **HABITAT AND HABITS** Semi-deserts, farmland, parks, gardens including in towns and villages, and archaeological sites. Partly diurnal. Appears squat when perched on the ground, boulders, or telegraph poles. Bobs head when agitated.

Long-eared Owl ■ *Asio otus* 36cm WS 94cm

DESCRIPTION Medium-sized, slim owl. Greyish-brown above, cryptically and finely barred and mottled. Pale buff below, with breast and belly streaked brown. Facial disk rufous-buff, with white 'eyebrows' down either side of centre and orange eyes. Ear-tufts long and held erect when alert. In flight long winged with yellow-buff on outer primaries and ear-tufts concealed. **VOICE** Quiet. Deep hoot and *rack rack* when alarmed. **DISTRIBUTION** In Egypt local winter visitor to north and Delta. Has bred. In Region local resident in Levant, where more widespread in winter south to northern Arabia. **HABITAT AND HABITS** Woodland and stands of trees including pines, copses, and plantations. Winter roosts in small groups. Nocturnal and crepuscular, feeding on small birds and mammals.

Short-eared Owl ▪ *Asio flammeus* 33–40cm WS 95–105cm

DESCRIPTION Medium-sized owl often active by day. Rather dark, heavily and coarsely streaked and mottled brown above. Buffish breast streaked brown, with pale belly sparsely

streaked more finely. Facial disk pale buff, with dark mask, white 'eyebrows', and very short ear-tufts. Eyes yellow. In flight very long winged, with white trailing edges and solid dark tips to primaries. Tail barred. **VOICE** Call rendered as hoarse *cheh-eh*. **DISTRIBUTION** In Egypt scarce winter visitor to north. Also on passage, including Sinai. In Region widespread but scarce winter visitor and on passage, but rare in south Arabia. **HABITAT AND HABITS** Open country, particularly marshy and wetland habitats, coastal flats, and pasture. Slow and elegant in flight, including by day, with wings held in shallow 'V'.

European Nightjar ▪ *Caprimulgus europaeus* 26cm WS 57cm

DESCRIPTION Cryptically patterned. Upperparts mottled greys, browns, blacks, and beiges – like tree-bark. Crown and nape grey. Pale band on lesser coverts. Tail banded. Bill tiny, gape large. In flight slender winged and long tailed; male only with white at bases of primaries and on tail. **VOICE** In flight, rattling, far-carrying *churr* at night. Calls *kru-ipp* or harsher *kwarr*. **DISTRIBUTION** In Egypt widespread but rarely scarce passage migrant. In Region on passage throughout – may breed in Syria. **Nubian Nightjar** *C. nubicus* much smaller and more rufous in southeastern Egypt, Naqab, and eastern Arabia. **HABITAT AND HABITS** Nocturnal and crepuscular. At rest highly camouflaged on the ground or perched along tree branch. When flushed note wing and tail pattern. Emerges at dusk, hawking for insects.

European Nightjar

Nubian Nightjar

Egyptian Nightjar ■ *Caprimulgus aegyptius* 26cm WS 56cm

DESCRIPTION Like slightly larger, paler version of European Nightjar (opposite). Mottled pale sandy-beige throughout, relieved by small white patch at neck-sides. Bill tiny, gape large. In flight, slender winged and long tailed; wings with darker, banded primaries. In male white tail corners and very little white in wing. **VOICE** Song repeated churrs rendered *kowrr kowrr kowrr*. **DISTRIBUTION** In Egypt breeding resident in Delta and Valley, and widespread in winter and on passage elsewhere. In Region widespread on passage throughout with few wintering. May breed Jordan and Syria. **HABITAT AND HABITS** Semi-deserts and desert margins. Nocturnal and crepuscular. In northern Egypt spends day roosting on desert floor, where highly cryptic, before emerging to hawk for insects at dusk.

Common Swift ■ *Apus apus* 18cm WS 44cm

DESCRIPTION Dark migrant swift. Very uniform, dark brown swift with small, pale throat-patch. Tail forked but often closed to a point in flight. In flight, typical scythe-like

wings, uniformly dark above with pale fringes to feathers only in juvenile. In flight, wing action very different from that of swallows, often with illusion that it is flying rapidly with one wing, then another. **VOICE** Highly vocal, with loud screams in wheeling flocks, especially at dusk. **DISTRIBUTION** In Egypt fairly common and widespread on passage – generally late in spring, early in autumn. Summer breeder in Levant. Widespread on passage throughout Region. **HABITAT AND HABITS** Largely urban, breeding in cities, towns, and villages. Anywhere on passage.

Pallid Swift ■ *Apus pallidus* 18cm WS 44cm

DESCRIPTION Very like Common Swift (above). Brown throughout, paler than Common and with more extensive pale throat-patch and paler lores and forehead contrasting with darker eye-patch. In flight back slightly darker, more contrast in wings,

and underside shows subtle scaling due to pale feather fringes. Flight much as Common's. **VOICE** Shrieks as Common's but slightly deeper. **DISTRIBUTION** In Egypt common resident in Delta and Valley (including central Cairo) and Western Oases. In Region summer breeder in parts of Levant, Arabia, and much of Gulf. **HABITAT AND HABITS** Largely urban, breeding in cities, towns, and villages. Also in 'natural' habitats such as desert gorges and cliffsides. Anywhere on passage.

Alpine Swift ■ *Apus melba* 21cm WS 57cm

DESCRIPTION Huge swift. Typical swift form
with scythe-like wings and cigar-shaped body –
but much larger. Uniform darkish brown above.
White throat separated from white underparts by
brown breast-band. Undertail-coverts and vent
brown. In flight deeper wingbeats than those of
Common and Pallid Swifts (opposite). **VOICE**
Protracted twittering or chattering rather than
shrieks of other swifts. **DISTRIBUTION** In
Egypt rather scarce passage migrant and winter
visitor mainly to Delta and Valley. In Region
summer breeder in Levant and parts of central
and southeastern Arabia. On passage over much
of Region. **HABITAT AND HABITS** Breeds in
mountainous areas, rocky gorges, and cliffs. Also
cities, towns, and villages. Anywhere on passage.

White-throated Kingfisher ■ *Halcyon smyrnensis* 28cm
(including bill 6cm) WS 42cm
(White-breasted Kingfisher,
Smyrna Kingfisher)

DESCRIPTION Large, striking kingfisher.
Upperparts and tail bright turquoise,
with head, belly, lesser coverts, and sides
chocolate-brown. Throat and breast white.
Huge bill bright red. Legs and feet red. In
flight largely bright blue with paler blue
wing-panel above. **VOICE** Very noisy. Loud
cackling call. Song high-pitched and loud
wittering *ti ti ti tu tu tu*, delivered from
prominent perch such as tree or aerial.
DISTRIBUTION Locally common resident
in northern Egypt even in central Cairo. Has
expanded range dramatically since the 1980s.
Locally in Lebanon, Israel, and Syria. Also
northern Gulf. **HABITAT AND HABITS**
Often found near water but not tied to
water. Irrigation canals, riversides, reedbeds,
farmland, and large gardens. Often perches
on wires overlooking paddies and fields in
agricultural areas.

Common Kingfisher ■ *Alcedo atthis* 17cm (including bill 4cm) WS 25cm
(Kingfisher)

DESCRIPTION Small, large-headed, short-tailed kingfisher. Bright blue-green above with reddish-orange underparts and cheeks. White throat and neck-patch. In flight back and tail

brilliant turquoise. Dagger-like bill all black (male) or with red base to lower mandible (female). Legs and feet red. **VOICE** Call high-pitched whistle, *tzee*. **DISTRIBUTION** In Egypt fairly common winter visitor throughout Delta and Valley and Western Oases, including Siwa. Also coasts including Mediterranean and Red Sea. Elsewhere in Region throughout in winter and on passage except southwest Arabia. **HABITAT AND HABITS** Waterside bird along rivers, streams, and irrigation canals, and in winter on coasts and in mangroves. Despite colors can be very cryptic perched in vegetation overlooking water. Often first view is flash of brilliant turquoise.

Pied Kingfisher ■ *Ceryle rudis* 25cm (including bill 5cm) WS 46cm

DESCRIPTION Large kingfisher. Black and white throughout with angular crest. Underparts white with one (male) or two (female) black breast-bands. In flight primaries

black with large white patch. Bill dagger-like and black. Legs and feet dark. **VOICE** Vocal, with sharp, rather high, rapid wittering, especially when in loose flocks. **DISTRIBUTION** In Egypt common resident throughout Delta and Valley, and Western Oases including Siwa. Range expansion in recent decades. Resident in Levant and also northern Gulf, spreading southwards in winter. **HABITAT AND HABITS** Tied to water. Along lakes, irrigation canals, and rivers, even in central Cairo. Also on coast. Habitually hovers over water before plunge diving for fish. Nests in mudbanks, sometimes in loose colonies.

Green Bee-eater

■ *Merops orientalis* 24cm (including tail projection 6cm) WS 30cm

(Little Green Bee-eater)

DESCRIPTION Small bee-eater, much smaller and slimmer than Blue-cheeked Bee-eater (below). Green throughout with black 'bandit' mask and variable black throat gorget. Egyptian race *cleopatra* has dull green throat and very long tail projections. Races *cyanophrys* and *muscatensis* have blue throats, browner on crown and shorter tail projections. Bill pointed and slightly downcurved. **VOICE** Rather high-pitched *prr-ip*, *prr-ip* in flight. **DISTRIBUTION** In Egypt race *cleopatra* common resident in Delta and Valley, including Fayoum. Races *cyanophrys* and *muscatensis* in eastern Arabia, north to Jordan and southern Levant, and Oman and UAE respectively. **HABITAT AND HABITS** Open country with trees, farmland, parks and gardens, and desert margins. Not in big flocks of other bee-eaters; often in pairs and singly. Makes forays for insects from perch such as wire or tree branch.

Blue-cheeked Bee-eater

■ *Merops persicus* 30cm

(including tail projection 6cm) WS 37cm

DESCRIPTION Large bee-eater, much larger than Green Bee-eater (above). Bright green to turquoise-green throughout, with yellow throat deepening to orange-chestnut. Black 'bandit' mask, bordered white and turquoise, and with white front. Bill pointed and

slightly downcurved. In flight, pointed wings, orange-brown below, and narrow, elongated central tail streamers. **VOICE** As European Bee-eater (p. 100) but coarser and higher pitched, delivered in flight. **DISTRIBUTION** Summer visitor to Egypt, breeding in Delta and northern Valley. Also Sinai. On passage throughout Region also localized summer breeder in Levant, northern Syria, and southeast Arabia. **HABITAT AND HABITS** Like European, on migration wheeling flocks most often located by call. Anywhere on passage, often roosting in reedbeds. Breeds colonially in burrows in sandbanks, irrigation ditches, and even archaeological sites.

Juvenile

European Bee-eater ■ *Merops apiaster* 28cm (including tail projection 3cm) WS 40cm

DESCRIPTION Brilliantly colored aerial bird. Harlequin colored with chestnut crown and mantle. Yellow on back. Turquoise below and on wings. Bright yellow throat bordered black and black 'bandit' mask. Bill pointed and slightly downcurved. In flight pointed wings, beige below, and narrow, elongated central tail streamers. **VOICE** On migration in flocks, constant *pruut, pruut pruut* in flight. **DISTRIBUTION** Migrating flocks common in Egypt in spring and autumn. Rare, occasional breeder in northeast Sinai. Common on passage throughout region, breeding in Levant, UAE, and Oman. **HABITAT AND HABITS** On migration wheeling flocks most often located by call. Often flies high but comes lower to feed. Hawks for large insects. Often perches on wires and aerials. Colonial nester in holes in sandbanks.

European Roller ■ *Coracias garrulus* 30cm WS 55cm

DESCRIPTION Like a small crow but brilliantly colored, especially in flight. Adult has turquoise-blue head, neck, and underparts. Turquoise and navy on wings and tail. Chestnut back and mantle. Bill dark, crow-like. In flight wings and tail deep indigo and turquoise.

VOICE Deep *rack rack*. More urgent, piercing *kreer kreer kreer* when agitated. **DISTRIBUTION** In Egypt scarce throughout on passage. Widespread throughout Region on passage, with very localized breeding in parts of Gulf and also Levant. **Abyssinian Roller** *C. abyssinicus* with long tail streamers and whiter face very rare in extreme southern Egypt; resident in southwest Arabia. **HABITAT AND HABITS** On passage in open country and farmland, acacia and palm groves in desert. Unobtrusive despite bright colors, but does perch on wires and exposed branches.

Indian Roller ▪ *Coracias benghalensis* 30cm WS 56cm

DESCRIPTION As European Roller (opposite) but browner and more mauve on head. Upperparts brown with bright turquoise on wings, crown, and belly. Cinnamon-mauve on cheeks, and throat streaked white. In flight wings and tail deep indigo and turquoise. Bill dark and heavy. **VOICE** Very vocal. Loud *rack rack*. Also loud *kreer kreer*, *kreer* when agitated or disturbed. **DISTRIBUTION** Not in Egypt. Resident in Oman (including Muscat) and northern Gulf, with some dispersal in autumn. **HABITAT AND HABITS** Open country, farmland, parks, and gardens. Loud and obvious, often perching in the open or in loose flocks with much interaction. Acrobatic flight in pursuit of large insects and in display, where dark blue/light blue pattern on wings and tail is obvious.

Hoopoe ▪ *Upupa epops* 27cm (including bill 5cm) WS 46cm

DESCRIPTION Very distinctive. Upperparts pale orange-pink; broadly banded black and white wings and white belly. Crest tipped black; normally held flattened but erected

when agitated or on alighting. Bill long, slender, and downcurved. Legs blue-grey. In flight note broad, rounded wings broadly barred black and white, white rump, and black tail with single white band. **VOICE** Song onomatopoeic, sonorous *oop oop oop*. Alarm *terrr* or *scheer*. **DISTRIBUTION** In Egypt common resident in Delta and Valley, North Coast, and Western Oases. Widespread on passage. In Region resident in Levant, south through western Arabia, and also southern Gulf. Widespread in winter and on passage. **HABITAT AND HABITS** Parks, gardens, farmland, orchards, and groves. Spends much time feeding on the ground

Eurasian Wryneck ■ *Jynx torquilla* 17cm
(Wryneck)

DESCRIPTION Cryptically patterned, aberrant woodpecker. Like a large warbler. Patterned like bark in greys, beiges, and browns not unlike a nightjar. Dark band from nape

down centre of back and dark eye-stripe. Pale below, barred dark with buffish throat. Bill short and pointed. In flight shows banded tail. **VOICE** Call sharp *teck*. Song more tuneful series of *vee vee vee …* **DISTRIBUTION** Uncommon passage visitor throughout Egypt. Occurs throughout Region on passage. **HABITAT AND HABITS** On migration in any area with cover. Farmland, scrub, parks and gardens, and even isolated acacia or palm groves. Unobtrusive when perched. More obvious when feeding on the ground, for example on ants, where tail often held raised. Twists neck at weird angles, especially when threatened, hence scientific name.

Black-crowned Sparrow-Lark ■ *Eremopterix nigriceps* 12cm
(Black-crowned Finch-Lark)

DESCRIPTION Very small, stout-billed lark. Short winged and short tailed. Male has brown upperparts and completely black underparts. Black head with white cheeks, ear-coverts, forehead, and nape. Bill short, conical, and pale blue-grey. Female uniform plain grey-beige; whitish below with pale grey, conical bill. In flight male all black below; female with black tail-sides and underwing-coverts. **VOICE** Calls include various twitters and short *chep*. Song delivered in low, circling display flight. **DISTRIBUTION** In Egypt resident, confined to southernmost regions of Eastern Desert. In Region resident but nomadic through much of west, south, and eastern Arabia, and throughout Gulf. **HABITAT AND HABITS** Semi-deserts, plains, scrubland, coastal dunes, and edges of cultivation. Feeds on the ground in small flocks.

Bar-tailed Lark

■ *Ammomanes cinctura* 14cm
(Bar-tailed Desert Lark)

DESCRIPTION Like Desert Lark (below), but smaller with different tail pattern. Small lark, uniform sandy-brown above with pale rufous on wings. Underparts pale whitish, unstreaked. Tail reddish-brown with clear, sharply demarcated, blackish tip. Bill smallish and pinkish. In flight shows dark tips to primaries. Similar **Dunn's Lark** *Eremalauda dunni* of Arabia, north to Naqab and south Syria, has heavier bill and dark sides to tail, not tip. **VOICE** Calls include *tschrr* and *see-oo*. **DISTRIBUTION** In Egypt in north, down Eastern Desert and Sinai. In Region resident over eastern Levant south through Naqab and northern Arabia and Gulf. More patchy farther south. **HABITAT AND HABITS** Flat or rolling deserts, sometimes very barren, and semi-deserts, avoiding rocky, mountainous areas.

Bar-tailed Lark

Dunn's Lark

Desert Lark ■ *Ammomanes deserti* 16cm

DESCRIPTION Most widespread and largest of the 'desert larks'. Uniform sandy-brown throughout but variable, *azizi* of east Arabia being very pale, *annae* of north Jordan dark. Unstreaked above with at best obscure streaking on breast. Obscure pale supercilium.

Dark tail grades smoothly to buffish tail-base. Bill yellowish, rather long, heavy, and pointed. In flight note more orange-brown edges to primaries. **VOICE** Quiet, but calls include soft *churr* or *dee-leeut*. **DISTRIBUTION** In Egypt common resident in Eastern Desert, desert margins of Delta and Valley, and throughout Sinai. In Region found over much of Levant south through Naqab and over much of Arabia and Gulf. **HABITAT AND HABITS** Rocky hillsides, wadi floors, and desert slopes. Usually solitary or in pairs.

Greater Hoopoe Lark ■ *Alaemon alaudipes* 18cm
(Hoopoe Lark)

DESCRIPTION Large, lanky lark. Uniform pale buff-brown above, including nape and crown, with much white on wings. Dark eye-stripe and pale supercilium. Dark moustachial stripe. Underparts whitish with spotting on breast. Bill long, slender, and downcurved. Legs long and pale. In flight wings strikingly black and white. Black tail with buff centre. **VOICE** Call *weerrp*. Song given in spectacular display flight, rapidly rising, then ebbing *dee dee dee dee* … **DISTRIBUTION** In Egypt common resident over much of north, Western Oases, Eastern Desert, and Sinai. In Region resident from eastern Levant and Naqab through entire Arabian peninsula including Gulf. **HABITAT AND HABITS** Flat sandy deserts and semi-deserts, including broad wadis and coastal dunes. Runs on the ground, periodically freezing. Generally single or in pairs.

Thick-billed Lark ■ *Ramphocoris clotbey* 17cm

DESCRIPTION Large lark with enormous bill. Thickset. Largely unstreaked grey-brown above; more rufous on wings. Head strongly patterned, with blackish ear-coverts and cheeks (with white spot) and down side of throat. White eye-ring. Underparts boldly spotted and streaked black. All markings darker in worn spring plumage. Female on average paler than male. Bill massive and very pale blue-grey. In flight note broad white trailing edges to dark wings. **VOICE** Whistling calls and *peep* or *swee*. Warbling song. **DISTRIBUTION** In Egypt rare in winter in northwest and also to Sinai. Status uncertain. In Region in Eastern Levant south to northern Arabia. **HABITAT AND HABITS** Flat, stony deserts in winter, dispersing to wadis, cultivated margins, and more rocky slopes. In small flocks, sometimes with other larks.

Bimaculated Lark ▪ *Melanocorypha bimaculata* 17cm

DESCRIPTION Large, thickset lark. Largely streaky-brown above with grey-brown back and rump. Head well patterned with white supercilium, dark loral and moustachial stripes, and brown cheeks. Underparts whitish with dark patch at breast-sides. Bill large, heavy,

Bimaculated Lark

Calandra Lark

and yellowish. In flight note short tail with white tip and brown-grey underside of wing. Similar, even larger **Calandra Lark** M. *calandra* has black underwing with white trailing edge. **VOICE** Twitters and short *tripp tripp*. **DISTRIBUTION** In Egypt scarce on passage in Sinai and Eastern Desert. In Region summer breeder in Levant. On passage through north and western Arabia with a few wintering. **HABITAT AND HABITS** Open scrub, semi-deserts, grassland, fields, and wasteland. On passage often in flocks.

Greater Short-toed Lark ▪ *Calandrella brachydactyla* 15cm
(Short-toed Lark)

DESCRIPTION Small, streaky, rather variable lark. Streaked grey-brown above including on crown, which may be tinged rufous. Face rather plain grey-brown with broad pale supercilium and brownish cheeks. Underparts pale whitish, unmarked save for generally small dark patch at breast-sides. Tail dark with white margins. Bill stout, pointed, and pale ivory. **VOICE** Calls include sharp *djirp* and *drrit*. **DISTRIBUTION** In Egypt widespread on passage throughout. Occasional in winter and may breed. In Region patchy summer breeder in Levant and Gulf. Much more widespread throughout on passage, and in winter in south. **HABITAT AND HABITS** Semi-deserts, plains, and open, cultivated areas. Often in small, dense flocks.

Lesser Short-toed Lark ▪ *Calandrella rufescens* 14cm

DESCRIPTION Very similar to Greater Short-toed Lark (p. 105) but greyer and more heavily streaked (only fractionally smaller). Streaked grey-brown above with whitish underparts finely to distinctly streaked on breast and without dark patch on sides. At

rest wing-tips clearly extend beyond tertials (barely so in Greater). **VOICE** Short *prrrrtt* in flight. Melodic song in rather fluttering, spiral display flight. **DISTRIBUTION** Local resident breeder in northern Egypt. More widespread across north and east, including Sinai on passage. In Region resident in much of Levant and more patchily in Gulf and eastern Arabia. Widespread on passage and in winter. **HABITAT AND HABITS** Semi-deserts, open stony scrub, salt flats, and cultivation. Often in flocks in winter and on passage.

Crested Lark ▪ *Galerida cristata* 18cm

DESCRIPTION The common crested lark over most of Region. Greyish-brown, somewhat streaked above on mantle and nape. Head has long, pointed crest, normally held erect. Underparts pale whitish with dark streaking on breast. Bill rather long and with decurved upper mandible. In flight note short dark tail with rufous margins, plain grey-brown rump, and rusty underwing with no white trailing edge. **VOICE** Rich song often delivered in flight. Calls include *doo-ee* and various whistles and mews. **DISTRIBUTION** In Egypt common resident in Delta, Valley, North Coast, and Sinai. In Region resident throughout except parts of central Arabia. **HABITAT AND HABITS** Semi-deserts, open country, grassland, and agricultural areas. Often seen around villages in wasteland and along roads and tracks. Fearless.

Eurasian Skylark ▪ *Alauda arvensis* 18cm
(Skylark, Common Skylark)

DESCRIPTION Greyish-brown above with dark streaking, and tertials with browner margins. Indistinct facial markings. Short, blunt crest often flattened. Pale buff-white below with dark streaking on breast. Pale, rather short, pointed bill. In flight differs from Crested Lark (opposite) in blackish tail with white margins, white trailing edges to wings, and pale underwings. **VOICE** Powerful, rolling, trilling song delivered in flight, often from great height. Calls include *preet* and *chiruup* when flushed. **DISTRIBUTION** In Egypt fairly common in winter and on passage, especially in north and Sinai. In Region widespread throughout in winter and on passage, although absent from western Arabia. **HABITAT AND HABITS** Cultivation, pastures, grassland, and open country, but not deserts. In winter often in flocks on stubble.

Temminck's Lark ▪ *Eremophila bilopha* 14cm
(Temminck's Horned Lark)

DESCRIPTION Adult a distinctive, boldly patterned lark. Very uniform bright rufous above greyer on nape and crown. Head black and white with black forecrown extending back to small 'horns', and black mask extending down cheek. White forehead, throat, and round cheeks. White underparts with black crescent across breast. Bill small, thin, and dark. In flight note blackish tail and dark tips to primaries. Juvenile lacks head markings. **VOICE** Various rather jingled calls. **DISTRIBUTION** Resident across northern Egypt except Delta and across north Sinai. In Region resident in east and west Levant from Syria south to Sinai border, northeastern Arabia, to northern Gulf. **HABITAT AND HABITS** Flat, open, stony and sandy deserts and semi-deserts. Usually solitary or in pairs.

Sand Martin ▪ *Riperia riperia* 12cm

DESCRIPTION Small martin with dull brown upperparts, including brown rump and tail. Underparts white with clear brown breast-band and white throat. Underwing brown with dark coverts. Tail has shallow fork. **VOICE** Persistent, rasping *trrrrrrr* and higher

chiiir when alarmed. **DISTRIBUTION** In Egypt common summer breeder throughout Delta and Valley. Widespread elsewhere on passage. Scarce in winter. In Region common passage migrant throughout, with a few wintering in southern Arabia. Has bred in Levant. **HABITAT AND HABITS** Breeds in colonies in burrows excavated in sandy cliffs and banks, often close to water. On passage widespread, especially over open country, grassland, marshes, and lakes and rivers. Perches on wires.

Rock Martin ▪ *Ptyonoprogne fuligula* 13cm
(Pale Crag Martin)

DISTRIBUTION Small pale, dull brown martin. Pale grey-brown upperparts, pale buff-grey underparts and throat with pale forehead. Tail barely forked and with small white spots visible when spread. In flight shows pale upperwing-coverts. Larger **Crag Martin** *P. rupestris* darker, with contrasting dark underwing-coverts and larger white spots on tail. **VOICE** Twittering and high *chp* or *trrit*. **DISTRIBUTION** In Egypt common resident in Valley margins south of Cairo, Western Oases, Eastern Desert, and south Sinai. In Region common resident from Naqab south through much of Arabia, to Oman and Gulf. Crag Martin breeding resident in Levant. Also on passage elsewhere. **HABITAT AND HABITS** Mountains, gorges, wadis, and ravines. Also at lower, more sandy elevations, in towns and villages.

Rock Martin

Crag Martin

Barn Swallow ■ *Hirundo rustica* 20cm (including tail streamers 5cm)

DESCRIPTION Dark, glossed steely-blue above. Forehead and throat dark red with blue-black breast-band. Underparts variable. In migrant races white below. In Egypt and Levant races *savignii* and *transitiva* brick-red below and on underwing-coverts. Slender, pointed wings and tail deeply forked, with long thin tail streamers and white spots when spread. **VOICE** Twittering song. Calls include sharp *vitt*. **DISTRIBUTION** In Egypt resident *savignii* very common in Delta and Valley. On passage throughout. In Levant *transitiva* common breeder.

Elsewhere widespread on passage and in winter. **HABITAT AND HABITS** Aerial over farmland, open country, and wetlands, and in cities, towns, and villages. Often perches on wires. Hawks for insects, sweeping to and fro along buildings. Nests on ledges, often on buildings.

Common House Martin ■ *Delichon urbicum* 14cm

(House Martin)

DESCRIPTION Short-tailed martin. Upperparts black, glossed dark blue on crown and back in good light. Underparts, including throat, white. White rump diagnostic. Tail black and moderately forked. Possible confusion with **Little Swift** *Apus affinis*, which has white rump but with dark brown underparts, pale throat, and square tail. **VOICE** Constant, rather conversational twittering, especially at colonies. **DISTRIBUTON** In Egypt common passage migrant throughout. In Region local summer breeder in Levant. On passage

throughout, with a few wintering in southern Arabia. **HABITAT AND HABITS** Open country and farmland, cities, towns, and villages. Often nests in roof eaves. Aerial but more fluttering in flight than Barn Swallow (above). Perches on wires. Collects mud for nest on the ground, when note fluffy white legs and feet.

Red-rumped Swallow ▪ *Cecropis daurica*
17cm (including tail streamers 4cm)

DESCRIPTION Similar to Barn Swallow (p. 109) but with slightly shorter tail streamers and reddish rump. Dark, glossed steely-blue above with rusty-brown cheeks and nape, and slaty crown. Pale buff below, subtly streaked, and with pale throat. Rump pale reddish. Slender, pointed wings with pale underwing-coverts and tail deeply forked with long tail streamers. Undertail-coverts black. **VOICE** Song low twitter. Calls include short *tweit*. **DISTRIBUTION** In Egypt widespread on passage but much less common than Barn. In Region local breeder in Levant, southwestern Arabia, and Oman. Widespread on passage throughout with a few wintering. **HABITAT AND HABITS** Nests on natural ledges, in caves or on buildings. Frequents open country, cliffs – inland and coastal – farmland towns, and villages.

Tawny Pipit ▪ *Anthus campestris* 17cm

DESCRIPTION Large, slim pipit. Plain sandy-brown above, barely streaked, and with dark centres to wing-coverts. Underparts whitish and largely unstreaked. Head rather pale with whitish supercilium, dark lores, and dark moustachial and thin malar stripes. Legs pale pink. Similar **Long-billed Pipit** *A. similis*, resident of rocky slopes in Levant and Arabia, has much buff on flanks and vent and lacks moustachial stripe. **VOICE** Calls include *tshilp* and short *chup*. **DISTRIBUTION** In Egypt widespread throughout on passage, and in winter scarce in Delta and Valley. In Region very local summer breeder in Levant. Widespread throughout on passage and in Arabia in winter. **HABITAT AND HABITS** Dry, open country, cultivation, sandflats, and semi-deserts. On the ground runs, stopping abruptly and standing erect.

Tawny Pipit

Long-billed Pipit

Meadow Pipit ■ *Anthus pratensis* 15cm

DESCRIPTION Typical pipit. Boldly streaked above with unmarked rufous-brown rump. Underparts off white, more buffish at sides and strongly streaked, including along flanks. Head has streaked crown and short pale supercilium, and narrow pale submoustachial stripe. Bill slender and yellowish. Hindclaw long and slightly curved. Very similar **Tree Pipit** *A. trivialis* has finer flank streaks, more warm buff below, and short hindclaw. **VOICE** Flight call rendered as *tsis-sip* or *sit-sii-sit*. **DISTRIBUTION** In Egypt common winter visitor to North Coast, Delta, and Sinai. In Region in winter and on passage through Levant, south to much of northern Arabia and Gulf. **HABITAT AND HABITS** Open country, farmland, marshes, and coast. Ground dwelling but not exclusively so.

Meadow Pipit

Tree Pipit

Red-throated Pipit ■ *Anthus cervinus* 15cm

DESCRIPTION Strongly marked pipit. Brown, heavily streaked blackish above, with whitish stripes on mantle. Underparts creamy-white, strongly streaked on upper breast and flanks. Pinkish-red throat in most adults, variably extending to supercilium, forehead, face, and breast. Paler in winter. In flight note brown rump with dark streaks. Bill fine with yellow base. Legs pinkish. **VOICE** High-pitched, thin *pseeee*. **DISTRIBUTION** In Egypt common on passage and fairly common in winter throughout. In Region winters through Levant and over much of Arabia and Gulf; scarcer in north. Widespread throughout on passage. **HABITAT AND HABITS** Generally wetter habitats including marshes, moist grassland, and cultivation. Breeds in High Arctic.

Water Pipit ■ *Anthus spinoletta* 16cm

DESCRIPTION Large, rather uniform pipit. Adult summer dull grey-brown above with largely unstreaked pale underparts variably suffused pinkish. In winter darker above with pale wing-bars; whitish below, tinged buff in Middle East race *coutellii*, with some dark streaking. Head has grey-brown crown and ear-coverts, clear cream-white supercilium,

and dark malar stripe. Legs often dark. In flight note broad white margins to tail. **VOICE** Call sharp *tsriii*. **DISTRIBUTION** In Egypt common in winter in north, Delta, northern Valley, and Sinai. In Region in winter and on passage through Levant south to northern Arabia, Gulf, and Oman. **HABITAT AND HABITS** Generally moist areas such as wetlands, grassland, farmland, and lake and river margins.

White Wagtail ■ *Motacilla alba* 18cm

DESCRIPTION Typical wagtail. Slender with long, slender tail constantly wagging. In winter largely grey and white, with grey back and rump, and darker crescent band on chest and white supercilium. Legs and bill dark. In summer and on passage male especially has head and neck boldly marked black and white. **VOICE** Common call *zee whit* or *zee zee whit*. Song rather simple twittering. **DISTRIBUTION** Often very common in winter and

on passage throughout Egypt and Region. Local breeder in Levant. **HABITAT AND HABITS** Variety of habitats, but generally close to water. Farmland, irrigation canals, marshes, riversides, pastures, villages and towns, and even city centres. Generally on the ground, where tail is wagged constantly. Walks busily. Flight deeply bounding, with long tail and white underparts clear in all plumages.

Yellow Wagtail ■ *Motacilla flava* 16cm

DESCRIPTION Small, relatively short-tailed wagtail. Many races found in Region, but all share yellow underparts, grey-brown to olive-brown upperparts with pale wing-bars, and dark tail with white margins. Head yellow *lutea*; yellow-green *flava*; grey *beema*; black *feldegg*. Pale supercilium may be present. Throat white to yellow, never dark. Legs and bill dark. Similar less common **Citrine Wagtail** M. *citreola* has all-yellow head in breeding male, greyish upperparts and pale arc around cheek in female and juvenile. **VOICE** Call variable *see-u*, but may be harsher or more metallic. **DISTRIBUTION** Fairly common passage and less common winter visitor to Egypt. Egypt race *pygmaea* common resident in Delta and Valley. In Region throughout on passage and in winter. **HABITAT AND HABITS** Found in marshes, wet pastures, agricultural land, and grassland including golf courses.

Citrine Wagtail

Yellow Wagtail

Grey Wagtail ■ *Motacilla cinerea* 19cm

DESCRIPTION Large wagtail. Slim and elegant with long, slender tail (proportionately much longer than Yellow Wagtail's, p. 113). Yellow below deepening to undertail-coverts. Grey above with wings darker and white margins to tertials. Head grey with white supercilium and in male dark on throat. Legs pinkish-brown (unique for wagtail in region). **VOICE** Metallic call *tzi-lit* or 'chink' in flight. **DISTRIBUTION** Fairly common passage and less common winter visitor to Egypt and throughout Region. Local resident

in northern Levant. **HABITAT AND HABITS** Tied to water and often found near fast-moving streams and rivers in hilly and mountainous areas, but also down to sea level and by lakes and ponds. Tail wagged very strongly and constantly. Makes aerial forays over water for insects, where white margins to tail are clear.

African Pied Wagtail ■ *Motacilla aguimp* 20cm

DESCRIPTION Large wagtail. Slender with long, slender tail. Entirely black and white. Black above with much white on wings. White below with black breast-band. Head black with white throat and white supercilium. Tail black with white margins. Legs and bill

dark. **VOICE** Whistling calls such as *tu-wee* and *tu tu tu*. **DISTRIBUTION** African species in Region confined to Egypt. Now resident on Lake Nasser and occasionally wanders farther north. **HABITAT AND HABITS** Waterside habitats including settlements, lakes, and rivers. On Lake Nasser on lake shores and rocky islets. When disturbed, flies a short distance with bounding flight and alights. Quite confiding.

White-spectacled Bulbul ■ *Pycnonotus xanthopygos* 20cm
(Yellow-vented Bulbul)

DESCRIPTION Like Common Bulbul (below), has dull grey-brown upperparts with darker hood and face, and short, angular crest. Paler grey-brown below with bright yellow vent. Tail dark brown. Eyes dark with white orbital ring. In flight as Common but note yellow vent. **VOICE** Very vocal. As Common. **DISTRIBUTION** In Egypt localized resident breeder confined to Sinai, especially south. In Region locally common resident from Levant, south through eastern and southern Arabia. Also southern Gulf to Oman. **HABITAT AND HABITS** Agricultural areas, palm groves, parks, gardens, and villages. In south Sinai in mountains and wadis, for example St Katherine's. Habits much as Common. Very vocal in small, noisy flocks.

Common Bulbul ■ *Pycnonotus barbatus* 20cm

DESCRIPTION Like a very large warbler. Dull grey-brown upperparts, with darker head and face, and short, angular crest. Paler grey-brown below with white vent. Tail dark brown. Eyes dark with no eye-ring. In flight rather long tailed, very uniform, and with no bars or streaks. **VOICE** Very vocal. Constant, rather musical warbling and chortling. Song loud, tuneful, and uneven. Also agitated *tchirrr*. **DISTRIBUTION** In Egypt only. Very common resident throughout Delta and Valley south to Aswan. Spreading west along North Coast. Replaced east of Suez Canal by White-spectacled Bulbul (above). **HABITAT AND HABITS** Agricultural areas, parks, gardens, towns and villages, and even large city centres. Despite dull colors, a confiding and easily seen bird. Social, often in small flocks and constantly calling.

White-eared Bulbul ■ *Pycnonotus leucotis* 18cm

DESCRIPTION Slightly smaller and more boldly marked than Common Bulbul (p. 115). Dull grey-brown upperparts, blackish head with slight crest, and large white cheek-patch. Underparts pale grey with yellow-orange vent. Tail dark brown with thin white tip. Eyes dark – no white orbital ring. **VOICE** Vocal. Tuneful jumblings much as Common's. **DISTRIBUTION** Absent Egypt. Local resident populations in northern Syria and northern Arabia (introduced). Also common resident throughout Gulf. Introduced species **Red-whiskered Bulbul** *P. jocosus* (tall black crest and red cheeks) and **Red-vented Bulbul** *P. cafer* (all-black head and scaly upperparts), both with red vents, now established in Gulf. **HABITAT AND HABITS** Farmland, parks, gardens, and even large city centres. Habits much as other bulbuls. Vocal and sociable.

White-eared Bulbul *Red-whiskered Bulbul* *Red-vented Bulbul*

Grey Hypocolius ■ *Hypocolius ampelinus* 23cm
(Hypocolius)

DESCRIPTION Unique, slim, and rather shrike-like. Male slender, pale blue-grey throughout, with long, black-tipped tail, and bold black mask, ear-coverts, and nape. Female similar but lacks black on head. Bill like a shrike's but without hook-tip. In flight both sexes grey-blue with white-tipped black primaries and long, black-tipped tail. **VOICE** Call mellow *whee-oo* or *whee-di-doo*. **DISTRIBUTION** Rare vagrant in Egypt, mostly to southeast. Winter visitor and on passage to much of Gulf, south to Oman and eastern Arabia. Sought-after regional specialty. **HABITAT AND HABITS** Woodland, scrub, palm groves, parks, and orchards. Attracted by fruiting trees. Not shy but skulking, often in flocks. When agitated may raise small crest.

Female *Male*

Rufous-tailed Scrub Robin ■ *Cercotrichas galactotes* 16cm

(Rufous Bush Robin, Rufous Bush Chat)

DESCRIPTION Warbler-like chat. Slim, and grey-brown above, dull pale-buff below. Bright rufous rump and tail. Tail often cocked, when black and white tips stand out. Head grey-brown, strongly patterned with dark eye-stripe and pale supercilium. Bill slender. Legs pinkish. In flight no wing-bars and note tail pattern. **VOICE** Rich and melodious song recalling thrush. Calls include sharp *teck* and thin *sseep* when agitated. **DISTRIBUTION**
In Egypt fairly common summer breeder along North and Red Sea Coasts, Sinai, Delta, Valley, and Western Oases. In Region on passage throughout and summer breeder to Levant, and Gulf to Oman. **HABITAT AND HABITS** Scrub, acacia groves, agricultural areas, parks, and gardens. Generally feeds on the ground, where note head and tail pattern – often associated with Prickly Pears.

Black Scrub Robin ■ *Cercotrichas podobe* 20cm

DESCRIPTION Distinctive dark, long-tailed chat. Adult sooty-black throughout; wings slightly browner. Tail long and graduated with white outer tips often cocked, revealing white tips to undertail-coverts. Bill slender and dark. Legs dark. **VOICE** Song similar to Rufous-tailed Scrub Robin's (above). Calls include melodic chattering. **DISTRIBUTION**
In Egypt increasingly regular on southern Red Sea coast with range expanding northwards. Vagrant southern Sinai. In Region common resident in eastern Arabia, where also expanding its range. **HABITAT AND HABITS** Desert margins, semi-deserts and scrub, acacia groves, agricultural areas, parks, hotel gardens, and golf courses. Rather shy, sticking to vegetation, often on the ground. Tail often cocked and fanned. Range expanding, probably as a result of hotel development providing suitable habitat.

European Robin ■ *Erithacus rubecula* 14cm
(Robin)

DESCRIPTION Small, distinctive chat. Uniform warm brown above. Face, throat, and upper breast orange-red bordered with silver-grey. Lower breast and belly whitish with brown flanks. Tail plain brown with warm brown rump. Bill small, thin, and pointed. Legs dark. Often appears large headed and rotund; at other times slim and longer necked. **VOICE** Powerful song. Calls include sharp *tick* and *tsiiih* when alarmed. **DISTRIBUTION** In Egypt fairly common winter visitor mainly to north, including Sinai, and Delta. In Region winter visitor to Levant south to northern Arabia and Gulf, where scarce. **HABITAT AND HABITS** Woodland, parks and gardens, farmland in winter, and also reedbeds and scrub. Secretive but not shy, often feeding on the ground, where droops wings and cocks tail.

Nightingale ■ *Luscinia megarhynchos* 16cm

DESCRIPTION Small, rather uniform thrush. Warm brown above, with brighter chestnut rump and tail. Grey-buff to buff underparts, with subtly paler throat. Dark eye with indistinct pale eye-ring. Legs pinkish. Very similar **Thrush Nightingale** *L. luscinia* darker, with less reddish on tail and rump and with faint mottling on breast. **VOICE** Renowned singer but song rarely heard on passage. Alarm whistled *heep*. **DISTRIBUTION** In Egypt fairly common on passage throughout. In Region summer breeding visitor to eastern Levant and widespread throughout on passage. A few may winter in southern Arabia. **HABITAT AND HABITS** Breeds in broadleaved woodland. On passage, woodland, areas of scrub, groves, parks, and gardens. Unobtrusive. When seen on the ground, often with tail raised and wings lowered.

Bluethroat ▪ *Luscinia svecica* 14cm

DESCRIPTION Rather dark, strongly patterned chat. Dark brown above; pale below with brown rump and rufous tail with broad dark tip. Head strongly marked with bold

white supercilium and moustachial stripe. Male has varying amounts of blue on throat with red or white (dependent on race) and narrow black border. Female has little or no blue. Bill slender. **VOICE** Call sharp *tack* or softer *hweet*. Song seldom heard in region. **DISTRIBUTION** In Egypt common on passage and in winter mainly in north. On passage throughout Region; generally rarer in winter. **HABITAT AND HABITS** Moist farmland, grassy areas, thickets, and gardens. Unobtrusive and often in thick cover, where strong head pattern best field mark. Feeds low in cover or on the ground, when tail often cocked.

Black Redstart ▪ *Phoenicurus ochruros* 15cm

DESCRIPTION Variable. Male dark grey on crown, nape, and mantle, sometimes paler on forehead, with dark brown wings sometimes with white panel. Below variable – blackish throughout with white on belly, black breast blending to reddish belly or sharply demarcated.

Female as Common Redstart (p. 120), but darker and greyer below. In flight both sexes show conspicuous rufous-red rump and tail. **VOICE** Calls include whistling *veest* and sharper *tik tik tik*. **DISTRIBUTION** In Egypt fairly common winter visitor and on passage in northern Delta and along North Coast. Rarer farther south. In Region local resident breeder in eastern Levant. On passage and in winter throughout. **HABITAT AND HABITS** As Common but generally in rockier habitats. Also cliffs, ruins, and villages. Shimmers tail like Common.

Common Redstart ▪ *Phoenicurus phoenicurus* 15cm

DESCRIPTION Male has uniform grey crown, nape, and mantle, and browner wings. Face and throat black with contrasting white forehead. Underparts reddish-orange, paler towards belly and vent. Female much more uniform grey-brown, and paler buff below. Both sexes have conspicuous rufous-red rump and tail. Legs dark. In flight note rufous tail; no white in wing. **VOICE** Call *hweet* and *tuk tuk tuk*. **DISTRIBUTION** In Egypt common on passage generally throughout. A few winter. In Region summer breeder in northern Levant. Widespread on passage throughout. **HABITAT AND HABITS** Breeds in mature woodland and parks. On passage wooded scrub, woodland, groves, and orchards. Hawks for insects from perch. Tail often shimmered and flirted, when bright rufous stands out.

Blackstart ▪ *Cercomela melanura* 15cm

DESCRIPTION Distinctive, all-grey desert chat. Uniform ash-grey above. Underparts whitish suffused grey on breast and with white throat. Tail all black. In flight plain grey above with black tail. No white on wings, tail, or rump. **VOICE** Clear, fluting song consisting of short, repeated phrases. Calls include *vee* when alarmed. **DISTRIBUTION** In Egypt confined to southern and eastern Sinai, where resident. Also very southeast and southwest of country. In Region resident from eastern Levant south through much of southern and eastern Arabia. **HABITAT AND HABITS** Mountains, cliffs, wadis, and rocky deserts, often with acacias and boulder fields. Active, with constant wing fanning, tail spreading, and flicking. Often feeds on the ground but also in acacias. Confiding and tame.

Whinchat ■ *Saxicola rubetra* 13cm

DESCRIPTION Streaky chat with distinctive head pattern. Male dark, streaked brown above including on crown, with white on primary coverts. Throat and underparts orange, becoming whitish on belly and vent. Dark cheeks with contrasting white supercilium and moustachial streak. Female paler and browner with buff supercilium. Legs dark. In flight tail brown with white sides at base; male has some white in wing. **VOICE** Call clicking *yu tek, yu-tek* or *yu tek tek* but generally silent on passage. **DISTRIBUTION** In Egypt fairly common throughout on passage. Widespread throughout Region on passage. **HABITAT AND HABITS** Plains, open country, farmland, fields, and lake shores. Appears rather upright when perched, swooping off to hawk insects.

European Stonechat ■ *Saxicola rubicola* 12cm
(Stonechat)

DESCRIPTION Small, big-headed chat. Male dark and heavily streaked above. Head entirely sooty-black. Incomplete white collar not meeting around back of neck. Underparts plain orange fading to pale buff on belly. Rump white or mottled. Bill dark, thin, and flycatcher-like. Female duller with brown head and more diffuse collar. **Eastern Stonechat** *S. maurus* has broader white collar, larger white rump, and orange restricted to small breast-patch. **VOICE** Short, twittering song. Calls include sharp *wheet trak-trak*.

DISTRIBUTION In Egypt fairly common winter visitor to north, Delta, and north Sinai. More widespread on passage. In Region in winter in Levant. Over much of Arabia and Gulf largely replaced by Eastern. **HABITAT AND HABITS** Open country, wasteland, scrub, and farmland.

Eastern Stonechat

European Stonechat

Northern Wheatear ■ *Oenanthe oenanthe* 15cm
(Wheatear)

DESCRIPTION Compact wheatear. Male has grey crown down mantle to back. Black wings, ear-coverts, mask, and lores, white supercilium, and pale pink-orange tinged underparts. Duller in autumn. Female has similar pattern but in browns and beiges. Both sexes have white rump and tail with black centre and terminal band. Less common **Isabelline Wheatear** *O. isabellina* very similar to female Northern, but note more upright stance and much broader terminal tail-band. **VOICE** Calls include whistled *heeet*

and harsher *tchack*. **DISTRIBUTION** In Egypt widespread on passage throughout. In Region very local summer breeder in Levant. Elsewhere widespread on passage. **HABITAT AND HABITS** Upland breeder. On passage to sea level in wide variety of open habitats, including farmland, orchards, and desert margins.

Northern Wheatear   *Isabelline Wheatear*

Eastern Black-eared Wheatear ■ *Oenanthe (hispanica) melanoleuca* 14cm
(Black-eared Wheatear)

DESCRIPTION Rather variable species. Male similar in pattern to Northern Wheatear (above), but more black and white and frequently with black throat. Sandy-white crown down mantle to back. Black wings, ear-coverts, mask, and lores, and whitish underparts.

Female has brown crown down mantle to back. Both sexes have white tail with black central stripe and terminal band broader at margins. In flight note tail pattern. **VOICE** Call like Northern's, *tchack* but also buzzy *bsscch*. **DISTRIBUTION** In Egypt widespread throughout on passage. Summer breeder through much of eastern Levant. Widespread throughout Arabia on passage, but largely absent from southeast. **HABITAT AND HABITS** Breeds in open, often rocky country with scattered trees and bushes. On passage open country including farmland, rough pastures, scrub, and stony slopes.

Desert Wheatear ▪ *Oenanthe deserti* 15cm

DESCRIPTION Compact, dark-throated wheatear. Male as Northern Wheatear (opposite) and Eastern Black-eared Wheatear (opposite), but sandy-brown on crown, nape, and mantle, with white scapulars contrasting with black wings and black throat. In winter has pale margins to wing and throat feathers. Female has weaker head pattern and paler throat.

In all plumages, especially in flight, note almost entirely black tail with whitish rump. **VOICE** Harsh *tchack* and more squeaky whistle. **DISTRIBUTION** Local resident breeder in Egypt along North Coast to Sinai. More widespread in winter and on passage. Resident breeder in Levant and northern Arabia. Widespread throughout Region in winter and on passage. **HABITAT AND HABITS** Breeds in semi-deserts with shrubs and open vegetation. On passage any open habitat such as farmland, pastures, and desert margins.

Female

Red-rumped Wheatear ▪ *Oenanthe moesta* 17cm

DESCRIPTION Large, large-billed wheatear. Male largely sooty-black above, with pale margins to tertials, secondaries, and especially coverts. Grey crown with whiter nape and forehead. Black face and throat. White breast and belly with orange-rufous undertail-coverts. In flight note all-dark tail and orange-rufous rump. Female pale grey-brown above with rufous head; uniform pale below. Broad dark tail-band and orange-rufous rump. **VOICE** Call short *prrit*. Song rather low pitched and trembling. **DISTRIBUTION** In Egypt scarce resident along North Coast west of Alexandria. In Region local resident in southeastern Levant, especially Jordan. **HABITAT AND HABITS** Semi-deserts and desert margins, salt flats, and desert cultivation such as Bedouin barley fields. Active on the ground, with tail-flicking and fanning, and bobbing.

Kurdish Wheatear ■ *Oenanthe xanthoprymna* 15cm
(Kurdistan Wheatear)

DESCRIPTION Breeding male has brown-grey back, mantle, nape, and crown. Blackish wings and black face with thin white supercilium. Underparts pale buff with black throat and rufous vent. In flight shows black and white tail with rufous rump. Female much

plainer drab grey-brown, with rufous tail with dark terminal band. **Red-tailed Wheatear** O. *chrysopygia*, previously considered conspecific, very like female Kurdish but with paler vent, paler wings, and pale underwing-coverts. VOICE Descending whistle and more abrupt *tchack*. DISTRIBUTION In Egypt scarce winter visitor to Delta margins, south Sinai, and Red Sea coast. In Region occasional in Levant. Red-tailed in winter in Gulf and Oman. HABITAT AND HABITS Barren rocky hillsides, screes, and boulder fields. Also cultivation and ruins.

Eastern Mourning Wheatear ■ *Oenanthe lugens* 15cm
(Mourning Wheatear)

DESCRIPTION Black and white wheatear. Upperparts black, including face and throat. White crown and nape. White rump and tail, with black terminal band and central stripe. Undertail-coverts orange. In flight note white panel on secondaries and primaries. **Pied Wheatear** O. *pleschanka* similar, but with white undertail-coverts and no white in wing. VOICE Calls include *tchuck tchuck* and harsher *tchack*. DISTRIBUTION In Egypt the most common 'pied' wheatear. Breeding resident along Valley and Eastern Desert to Sinai. In Region resident breeder in Levant and northern Arabia. On passage in eastern Arabia and Gulf. HABITAT AND HABITS Mountains and rocky slopes, gorges and wadis, deserts, and semi-deserts. Several similar species, but note orange undertail-coverts and white in wing.

Eastern Mourning Wheatear

Pied Wheatear

Hooded Wheatear ■ *Oenanthe monacha* 17cm

DESCRIPTION Large, slim, long-billed wheatear. Sexes differ. Male a large, slim wheatear, with black upperparts, face, and throat to breast. Extensive white crown and white underparts (much more extensive white than in White-crowned Wheatear, below), back, and rump. Tail largely white with black centre only. Female grey-brown with paler underparts, and pale buff rump and tail with no terminal band. **VOICE** Song less musical than White-crowned's. Calls include repeated *jirrp* and thinner *wheet-wheet* ... **DISTRIBUTION** In Egypt resident along Valley margins, Eastern Desert, and southern Sinai. In Region resident from Naqab patchily south through Arabia to Oman and southern Gulf. Some dispersal in winter. **HABITAT AND HABITS** Rocky deserts, mountains, crags, and wadis. In Sinai down to coast. Often hawks for insects in flight. Not shy but unobtrusive.

White-crowned Wheatear ■ *Oenanthe leucopyga* 17cm
(White-crowned Black Wheatear)

DESCRIPTION Large desert wheatear. Black throughout with white on crown and lower belly, vent, and undertail-coverts. Tail largely white with black centre and spots at corners. Immature birds often lack white on crown. In flight black with white crown and largely white rump and tail. **VOICE** Vocal. Song characteristic sound of deserts. Rich whistling, often mimetic, with softer subsong. Calls include *peet peet*. **DISTRIBUTION** In Egypt common resident in Eastern, Western, and Sinai deserts and Western Oases. In Region resident from Naqab, south through western Arabia; locally farther east. **HABITATS AND HABITS** Barren, generally rocky deserts, mountains, cliffs, and wadis. Can be found in very remote areas, but also familiar in and around oases, as at Siwa.

Rufous-tailed Rock Thrush ▪ *Monticola saxatilis* 19cm
(Common Rock Thrush)

DESCRIPTION Smallish, long-billed thrush. Male blue-grey above with blackish wings and white back. Rufous-orange below. More scalloped in winter. Female scaly blue-grey above and scaly buff below. Both sexes have slim, straight bill and short, rufous tail. **VOICE** Song musical, similar to Blackbird's (opposite). Calls include sharp *chack*. **DISTRIBUTION** In Egypt fairly common on passage, especially in east of country. Widespread on passage throughout Region. Very local summer breeder in northern Levant. **HABITAT AND HABITS** Mountains, dry highlands, wadis, and rocky areas, including ruins. On passage also at much lower altitudes. Female unobtrusive, and male can be hard to see despite colors, but white back shows well in flight. Female paler and 'scalier' than female Blue Rock Thrush (below).

Blue Rock Thrush ▪ *Monticola solitarius* 22cm

DESCRIPTION Slim, long-billed thrush. Male appears all dark at distance; actually dark blue, more scalloped in winter, with blackish-brown wings and tail. Female dark grey-blue above; paler below with extensive dark barring. Bill straight and slender. Legs dark. **VOICE** Song like Blackbird's (opposite) with long pauses. Call hard *chak* or softer *heeed*. **DISTRIBUTION** In Egypt fairly common on passage and in winter throughout Sinai and eastern Egypt, from Cairo south through Eastern Desert. In Region resident breeder in Levant and on passage, and in winter throughout. **HABITAT AND HABITS** Mountains, wadis, and cliffs, but also to sea level, for example in north Sinai. Locally towns and villages. Appears all dark at distance but profile distinctive with the long bill. Often perches in the open.

Female   *Male*

Blackbird ■ *Turdus merula* 25cm
(Eurasian Blackbird, Common Blackbird)

DESCRIPTION Male black throughout with contrasting bright yellow bill and orbital ring. Legs dark. Female dark brown, slightly paler below and on throat, and heavily streaked. Bill dark yellowish; legs dark. Juvenile more speckled. **VOICE** Fabulously rich, mellifluous song, often delivered from prominent perch. Alarm ascending *chack chack* or more subdued *chk chk chk*. **DISTRIBUTION** In Egypt now common breeding resident over much of north, Delta and northern Valley, and Western Oases. Winter visitor in north. In Region resident breeder in Levant south to north Sinai. Winter and passage south to northern Arabia and Gulf. **HABITAT AND HABITS** Agricultural areas, palm groves, orchards, parks, and gardens. Great range expansion in Egypt, including to central Cairo. Normally feeds on the ground.

Zitting Cisticola ■ *Cisticola juncidis* 11cm
(Fan-tailed Warbler)

DESCRIPTION Similar to Graceful Prinia (p. 128) but note short tail. Small, rotund warbler; pale brown, heavily streaked dark above, including on nape and crown, contrasting with plain 'face'. Rump rusty orange-brown. Tail short, with black and white tips obvious in flight from below.

Whitish throat and plain pale buff underparts. Thin bill dark in male, pale in female. Legs pinkish. **VOICE** Song incessant *zip zip zip zip …* Call *chipp*. **DISTRIBUTION** In Egypt common resident throughout Delta and Valley to Fayoum. In Region resident in eastern Levant and southeastern Arabia. **HABITAT AND HABITS** Farmland, open country, fields, and pastures. Most often located in bounding, circling display flight, where its song can be a characteristic sound of rural areas.

Graceful Prinia ▪ *Prinia gracilis* 11cm

DESCRIPTION Tiny, mouse-like warbler. Streaky-brown upperparts to nape and crown. Plain grey-brown cheeks, pale throat and underparts unstreaked, and with flanks flushed

browner. Rump brown. Tail long, slender, and graduated, dark above and with white tips below; frequently cocked. Bill dark; paler in summer. Legs pinkish. **VOICE** Very vocal. Song incessant *prrrlip prrrlip prrrlip*. Calls include loud *tsit* and longer *srrrrt*. **DISTRIBUTION** In Egypt common resident throughout Delta and Valley, and across to west Sinai. In Region widespread common resident throughout Levant and Arabia, including Gulf. **HABITAT AND HABITS** Open scrub, farmland, parks and gardens, wasteland, and greenery in towns and villages. Often located by sound. Not shy but difficult to see and rather skulking.

Levant Scrub Warbler ▪ *Scotocerca inquieta* 10cm
(Scrub Warbler)

DESCRIPTION Tiny, wren-like warbler. Plain brown above but with streaked crown. Broad, whitish to pale supercilium with contrasting dark eye-stripe and dark eye. Underparts pale, streaked brown. Tail long and slender, dark above and dark below, with narrow pale tips. Often cocked. Legs dark pink. **VOICE** Calls include two-syllable,

descending *wee wew* and more extended trill. **DISTRIBUTION** In Egypt resident restricted to eastern margins of Delta and Valley, Eastern Desert, and Sinai. In Region resident over central and southern Levant, northern and western Arabia, through south to southern Gulf. **HABITAT AND HABITS** Deserts and semi-deserts, wadis, rocky plains, and hillsides. Drier country than similar Graceful Prinia (above). Active, often singly or in pairs, feeding on the ground at bases of plants.

Savi's Warbler ▪ *Locustella luscinioides* 14cm

DESCRIPTION Skulking warbler generally
in thick cover. Superficially like Eurasian
Reed Warbler (p. 131), being uniform greyish
olive-brown above, continuous with rump and
graduated tail. Indistinct pale supercilium.
Underparts pale buff with whitish throat.
Undertail-coverts long and full; uniform pale
rusty-brown with suggestion of dark tips. **VOICE**
Song monotonous reeling. Call metallic *pitch*.
DISTRIBUTION In Egypt uncommon on passage
on broad front including Sinai. In Region very
local summer breeder and on passage in Levant.
Locally on passage in northern Arabia and Gulf.
HABITAT AND HABITS Breeds in reedbeds.
On passage in variety of damp, vegetated
habitats, including marshes, riverbanks, and
stands of dank vegetation. Often forages on the
ground or clambers low in vegetation.

Eastern Olivaceous Warbler ▪ *Iduna pallida* 13cm
(Olivaceous Warbler)

DESCRIPTION Like a greyish Eurasian Reed
Warbler (p. 131), but with square-ended tail.
Drab olive-grey above, pale buffish underparts,
and whitish throat. Head pointed, and rather
plain with dark lores, short pale supercilium,
and pale eye-ring. Wing may have pale panel.
Tail olive-grey with pale margins and square
end. Bill longish and pointed, with yellowish
lower mandible. Legs pale grey-brown. **VOICE**
Rambling, 'cheerful' song interspersed with
harsher, scratchy notes. Calls include sharp
tchek. **DISTRIBUTION** In Egypt common
summer breeder in Delta, Valley, Sinai, and
Western Oases. Widespread on passage. In
Region summer breeder in Levant, Gulf,
and, patchily, parts of Arabia. Widespread on
passage. **HABITAT AND HABITS** Woodland,
orchards, palm groves, scrubland, and oases.
Any vegetation on passage. Characteristically
pumps tail downwards.

Sedge Warbler ▪ *Acrocephalus schoenobaenus* 13cm

DESCRIPTION Small, streaky *Acrocephalus*. Brown above, streaked dark on back and mantle. Plain, warm brown rump. Streaked brown crown and cheeks, with broad pale buff supercilium contrasting with dark lores. Underparts buffish, paler on throat and towards belly. Similar **Moustached Warbler** *A. melanopogon* has blackish crown, white supercilium, and greyish ear-coverts. **VOICE** Song similar to Eurasian Reed Warbler's (opposite). Calls include sharp *chek*. **DISTRIBUTION** In Egypt common and widespread throughout on passage. In Region widespread throughout on passage, with a few in winter in Arabia. Moustached very localized resident in Levant and northeastern Arabia and Gulf. **HABITAT AND HABITS** Generally in damp stands of vegetation, including marshes, reedbeds, and waterside thickets. On passage also in drier habitat.

Sedge Warbler

Moustached Warbler

Marsh Warbler ▪ *Acrocephalus palustris* 13cm

DESCRIPTION Very similar to Eurasian Reed Warbler (opposite), but note overall brown plumage with slight olive tinge, warmer on rump but less rusty than in Eurasian Reed. Pale margins to flight feathers and especially tertials. Bill slightly shorter and blunter – 'stronger'. Indistinct buffish supercilium and pale eye-ring. Underparts off white with yellowish cast. **VOICE** Song much more musical and fast-moving than Eurasian Reed's, with extensive mimicry. Calls include *chek* and longer *terrr*. **DISTRIBUTION** In Egypt widespread through Delta and Valley on passage. In Region widespread throughout on passage. **HABITAT AND HABITS** Areas of dank vegetation, waterside bushes, and irrigation ditches. On passage more diverse habitats.

Eurasian Reed Warbler ▪ *Acrocephalus scirpaceus* 13cm

DISTRIBUTION Common warbler of damp habitats. Upperparts uniform warm brown, with more rusty tinge to rump. Rather pointed head with long, slender bill, and indistinct pale supercilium that does not extend behind eye. Race *fuscus* of Middle East has pale underparts with buff tinge and slightly greyer upperparts. **VOICE** Calls include *che* or *chk*. Song 'chatty' and 'jittery', with some mimicry – monotonous. **DISTRIBUTION** In Egypt very local summer breeder in Delta and Valley. Widespread on passage. In Region patchy summer breeder in Levant south to northern Arabia and Gulf. Widespread throughout on passage, with a few wintering in southern Arabia. **HABITAT AND HABITS** Breeds in reedbeds and vegetated areas at water margins. On passage in more diverse habitats.

Clamorous Reed Warbler ▪ *Acrocephalus stentoreus* 18cm

DESCRIPTION Very large warbler, a third again larger than Eurasian Reed Warbler (above). Uniform dull brown to olive-brown above; paler below with whitish throat and narrow pale eyebrow. Bill distinctive, long and narrow. Similarly sized **Great Reed Warbler** *A. arundinaceus* warmer brown above with heavier bill. **VOICE** Very vocal, with variety of loud *chacks* and *krrrs*. Song gruff and croaking. Loud. **DISTRIBUTION** Common resident in Egypt in Delta and all along Nile Valley and west to Suez Canal. Also some Western Oases. Locally in suitable habitat throughout Region, including Gulf to Oman. **HABITAT AND HABITS** Listen out for calls in areas of reedbeds, even isolated clumps; also maize and cane fields in vicinity of water.

Olive-tree Warbler ■ *Hippolais olivetorum* 17cm

DESCRIPTION Huge version of Eastern Olivaceous Warbler (p. 129). Very large, and mainly grey above and whitish below. Primaries blackish with long projection. Tertials with pale margins forming pale wing-panel. Head flattish (though may raise crown), and grey with white eye-ring and whitish lores. Tail blackish with white margins. Bill powerful, long, and yellowish. Legs grey. **VOICE** Harsh song not unlike deeper version of

Eastern Olivaceous's. Calls include agitated *tac tac*. **DISTRIBUTION** In Egypt generally very scarce on passage in Delta, east, and Sinai. In Region summer breeder in Levant south to northern Naqab. On passage also to northern Arabia. **HABITAT AND HABITS** Woodland, olive groves, scrub, and parkland. On passage any vegetation, including vegetated wadis, for example in south Sinai. Characteristically dips and spreads tail.

Icterine Warbler ■ *Hippolais icterina* 13cm

DESCRIPTION Like Eastern Olivaceous Warbler (p. 129), but dull grey-green above with pale margins to tertials and secondaries creating pale wing-patch. Long primary extension. Underparts uniform pale yellow. Head has pale lores, pale yellow supercilium, and pale eye-ring. Often shows peaked crown with feathers raised. Bill pointed and pale

pinkish-yellow. Legs bluish-grey. **VOICE** Trisyllabic call rendered *de te roy*. Also short *chek*. **DISTRIBUTION** In Egypt scarce on passage mainly along North Coast, east, and Sinai. In Region on passage mainly in Levant, and occasionally in Gulf. **HABITAT AND HABITS** Woodland, orchards, groves, parks, and gardens. Generally keeps to canopy, when can be hard to see in dappled foliage.

Eastern Subalpine Warbler ■ *Sylvia (cantillans) albistriata* 12cm

DESCRIPTION Small *Sylvia* warbler. Male uniform blue-grey above, browner on wings. Head blue-grey with prominent white moustachial stripe. Throat and breast brick-red; underparts pale, suffused pinkish. Tail grey with white margins. Red eye-ring. Female browner above, pale pinkish-buff below and on throat, with suggestion of white moustache, and with pale eye-ring. **VOICE** Fast, scratchy song. Calls include *tek*, sometimes repeated. **DISTRIBUTION** In Egypt widespread scarce to common on passage. May winter. On passage in Levant, Naqab, and northwestern Arabia. **HABITAT AND HABITS** Light woodland, scrub, thickets, and on passage oases and acacia groves. Rather skulking warbler, and brick-red throat and breast can be difficult to see in dense cover.

Sardinian Warbler ■ *Sylvia melanocephala* 13cm

DESCRIPTION Male has grey upperparts with paler margins to tertials and grey rump. Head black with bright red eye-ring and contrasting white throat. Underparts pale grey. Tail blackish with bold white tips clear in flight. Legs pinkish. Female browner with grey head, duller eye-ring, and buffish underparts. **VOICE** Song rapid chattering. Calls include sharp *tcheck*. **DISTRIBUTION** In Egypt resident in northeast Sinai, but widespread and common throughout in winter and on passage. In Region resident in Levant, dispersing in winter. Similar **Ménétriés Warbler** *S. mystacea* has pinkish underparts and throat in male; scarce on passage throughout. **HABITAT AND HABITS** Breeds in woodland and open country with bushy scrub. In winter also desert margins, wadis, and oases. Restless, often flicking wings and tail.

Sardinian Warbler

Ménétriés Warbler

Rüppell's Warbler ■ *Sylvia rueppelli* 13cm

DESCRIPTION Distinctive *Sylvia* warbler. Male darkish, uniform grey above with pale margins to tertials and secondaries. Crown, face, and throat black (diagnostic), with white moustachial stripe. Prominent dark red eye-ring. Underparts pale grey. Dark tail with white margins. Female paler, with pale throat and fainter, browner eye-ring. Legs reddish-brown. Similar **Cyprus Warbler** *S. melanothorax* has white underparts, including throat, extensively spotted and scaled with black in both sexes. **VOICE** Song similar to Sardinian Warbler's (p. 133). Typical call sharp *zack*. **DISTRIBUTION** In Egypt fairly common and widespread on passage. On passage in Levant to northern Arabia. Cyprus rare on passage in Sinai and Levant. **HABITAT AND HABITS** On passage open country with scrub and bushes, acacia groves, and gardens.

Rüppell's Warbler

Cyprus Warbler

Asian Desert Warbler ■ *Sylvia nana* 12cm

DESCRIPTION Small, pale *Sylvia* warbler. Sexes alike. Pale grey-brown above with more golden tinge to wings, darker primaries, and contrasting dark alula. Underparts whitish with white throat. Iris pale with pale eye-ring and whitish lores. Bill yellowish. Tail and

rump warm buff-orange with darker central rectrices and extensive white margins. Legs pale yellow. **VOICE** Call chatter rendered *cherrrr rr rr rr*. Song more trilling. **DISTRIBUTION** In Egypt only regular in winter in Sinai, especially wadis in south. In Region in winter and on passage over much of Arabia, Gulf, and southern Levant. **HABITAT AND HABITS** Deserts and semi-deserts, scrub, wadi floors, and plains. Most often on the ground, scuttling between and around low vegetation. Active.

Arabian Warbler ■ *Sylvia leucomelaena* 15cm

DESCRIPTION Large warbler, near endemic to Region. Largely uniform grey-brown above, paler in race *Naqabensis*. Head blackish with thin pale eye-ring. Iris dark. Throat bright white with underparts more dusky. White undertail-coverts. Tail longish, slightly graduated, and appearing all black (actually with obscure white tips). **VOICE** Song clear and mellifluous. Call short *tcha-tcha* and short rattle. **DISTRIBUTION** In Egypt resident in very southeast, and possibly in winter in southern Sinai. In Region resident in Naqab (race *naqabensis*), and in western and southwestern Arabia. **HABITAT AND HABITS** Semi-deserts, wadi floors, and acacia groves. Shy and unobtrusive in canopy, although sings from open perch. Often dips tail as it skulks through foliage.

Eastern Orphean Warbler ■ *Sylvia crassirostris* 15cm

DESCRIPTION Large *Sylvia* warbler. Male like Sardinian Warbler (p. 133), but considerably larger and with paler grey mantle extending to nape and dark-grey crown contrasting with darker ear-coverts. Clear white throat and pale buff underparts tinged pink. Tail dark with white margins. Pale iris. Female similar but with grey crown and dark iris. Stout bill. Legs dark. Similar **Barred Warbler** *S. nisoria* has dark-barred underparts and white wing-bars. **VOICE** Contact call brief *tech*. Also more prolonged rattle. **DISTRIBUTION** In Egypt rare on passage, mainly in eastern part of country and Sinai. In Region summer breeder in Levant and widespread throughout on passage. Some winter in east Arabia. **HABITAT AND HABITS** Bushy scrub, plantations, orchards, acacia groves, and parks.

Eastern Orphean Warbler

Barred Warbler

Lesser Whitethroat

Lesser Whitethroat
■ *Sylvia curruca* 12cm

DESCRIPTION Small, compact *Sylvia*. Dull brown above with dark grey cap, blackish ear-coverts, and contrasting white throat. Underparts pale buff. Tail rather short, and dark with no white margin, and unmarked pale undertail-coverts. Legs dark. Differs from Common Whitethroat (as below); also note absence of rusty margins to wing feathers. Smaller, paler **Desert Whitethroat** *S. minula* in winter and on passage in southern Arabia and Gulf. **VOICE** Song loud rattle. Calls include sharp *tek*. **DISTRIBUTION** In Egypt widespread and common throughout on passage. In Region summer breeder in Levant. On passage throughout and in winter in south Arabia. **HABITAT AND HABITS** Trees, acacia groves, dense scrub, orchards, and plantations. Desert in drier country, semi-deserts, and wadi floors. Can be very numerous on passage.

Desert Whitethroat

Common Whitethroat ■ *Sylvia communis* 14cm

DESCRIPTION Larger and more rufous than Lesser Whitethroat (above) – also note pale legs. Male has brownish upperparts with clear chestnut margins to flight feathers. Head, nape, and mantle grey with white eye-ring. Throat bright white with pinkish-buff underparts. Tail dark with white margins. Female much browner, with race *icterops* over much of Arabia with little chestnut. Legs yellowish. Similar **Spectacled Warbler** *S. conspicillata* has black lores and more uniform chestnut wings. **VOICE** Fast, warbling song. Call coarse *whedt whedt whedt*. **DISTRIBUTION** In Egypt common and widespread on passage. In Region local summer breeder in Levant. On passage throughout with a few wintering in southern Arabia. **HABITAT AND HABITS** Scrub, and patchy, open country with hedges and shrubs.

Common Whitethroat

Spectacled Warbler

Garden Warbler ■ *Sylvia borin* 14cm

DESCRIPTION Lack of features is the main feature. Sexes alike. Dull grey-brown above, including rump and tail. Paler buff below. Suggestion of supercilium and in good light; obscure grey patch at neckside. No white bars in wings or margins to tail. Bill rather short. Iris dark. Legs darkish. **VOICE** Rattling call and short, repeated *chek* when alarmed. **DISTRIBUTION** In Egypt fairly common on passage throughout, including Sinai. In Region widespread throughout except for southeastern Arabia. **HABITAT AND HABITS** On passage any area with trees and bushes, including open woodland, scrub, farmland parks, and large gardens.

Blackcap ■ *Sylvia atricapilla* 14cm

DESCRIPTION Rather plain, capped warbler. Sexes differ. Male uniform grey-brown above and paler grey below. Tail darker. No white bars in wings or margins to tail. Matt black cap. Iris dark. Legs darkish. Female has rufous cap. **VOICE** Call hard *teck* repeated when agitated. **DISTRIBUTION** In Egypt fairly common winter visitor to northern Egypt, including north Sinai, and common on passage elsewhere. In Region local breeder in Syria and winter visitor to Levant, where also on passage. Passage throughout Arabia, some wintering. **HABITAT AND HABITS** Breeds in broadleaved woodland. Otherwise woodland, scrub, farmland, orchards, groves, and parks. In Levant possible confusion with **Sombre Tit** *Parus lugubris*, which has whitish cheeks and black throat.

Blackcap

Sombre Tit

Eastern Bonelli's Warbler ■ *Phylloscopus orientalis* 12cm

DESCRIPTION Fairly two-tone *Phylloscopus*. Upperparts with mantle and head greyish-brown, tertials dark-edged pale yellow-green, and flight feathers with yellow margins. Rump bright green, and tail dark with yellow-green feather margins. Head quite plain, with indistinct pale supercilium and dark lore and eye-stripe. Ear-coverts pale brown. Bill pink-brown with darker tip. Legs dark grey. **VOICE** Call short *chip*. **DISTRIBUTION**

In Egypt fairly common on passage, especially in north and east, and Sinai. In Region very local breeder in Levant. On passage from Levant through to northern Arabia. **HABITAT AND HABITS** Woodland, scrub, acacia groves, and parkland. On passage any area of vegetation. Active, searching for insects among foliage. Often hovers, when green rump a useful feature.

Wood Warbler ■ *Phylloscopus sibilatrix* 13cm

DESCRIPTION Region's brightest and yellowest *Phylloscopus*. Upperparts uniform clean moss-green with slight greyish cast. Long primary projection gives long-winged appearance. Below sharply demarcated, clean white, with bright yellow ear-coverts, throat, and breast-sides. Head has long, broad, and strongly yellow supercilium, contrasting with dark eye-

stripe. Bill pinkish-yellow with darker tip. Legs pinkish. **VOICE** Call sharp *zip* but generally quiet on passage. **DISTRIBUTION** In Egypt widespread on passage but less common than Willow Warbler (opposite). In Region widespread on passage in Levant, Gulf, and southern Arabia, where scarce. **HABITAT AND HABITS** Woodland with tall trees, scrub, acacia groves, and parkland. On passage any area of vegetation. Often in canopy.

Chiffchaff ■ *Phylloscopus collybita* 11cm
(Common Chiffchaff)

DESCRIPTION Similar to Willow Warbler (below) but slightly smaller and browner. Variable, with several races in Region. Brownish-green above with slight grey tinge. Pale below with slight buffish to yellowish tinge; paler in race *abientinus* with whiter undertail-coverts. Head has short, faint pale supercilium and dark eye-stripe separating pale eye-ring. Bill dark with yellow at base.

Legs dark. **VOICE** Song *chiff-chaff chiff-chaff chiff-chaff*. Calls include soft *hweet* or *peep*. **DISTRIBUTION** In Egypt common in winter throughout Delta and Valley, North Coast, and Sinai. Widespread on passage. In Region resident in northern Levant. Widespread throughout in winter and on passage. **HABITAT AND HABITS** Woodland, scrub, groves, plantations, and parkland. When foraging often dips tail. Only *Phylloscopus* widespread and common in Region in winter.

Willow Warbler ■ *Phylloscopus trochilus* 12cm

DESCRIPTION Like Chiffchaff (above), but with more greenish-tone. Upperparts greyish brown-green. Pale below, including throat, with yellow tinge to strongly suffused yellow in some autumn birds. Head has moderately long pale supercilium and dark eye-stripe and lores showing more patterning than Chiffchaff's. Bill slightly longer and with more pink/yellow.

Legs generally pinkish. **VOICE** Common call disyllabic, ascending *hew-lit*. **DISTRIBUTION** In Egypt widespread and common throughout on passage, including remote oases. In Region common on passage throughout. **HABITAT AND HABITS** Woodland, scrub, acacia groves, and parkland. On passage any area of vegetation. On passage only; winters in sub-Saharan Africa.

Spotted Flycatcher ▪ *Muscicapa striata* 15cm

DESCRIPTION Relatively plain, chat-like bird with distinctive jizz. Uniform grey-brown above; pale below streaked brown on chest, forehead, and crown. Pale throat with streaked margins. Pale margins to primaries but no white wing-bars. Bill slender and pointed. Eye dark with indistinct pale orbital ring. Behavior distinctive. **VOICE** Simple, rather

'scratchy', high-pitched song. Call short, sharp *tzeet*. **DISTRIBUTION** In Egypt widespread on passage throughout. Local summer breeder in Levant and widespread throughout as passage migrant. **HABITAT AND HABITS** Parks, gardens, and woodland margins. On passage any area with trees and scrub, even remote oases, for example in Western Desert. Often perches in the open, upright and flicking wings. Flies out hawking for insects, often returning to same perch.

Red-breasted Flycatcher ▪ *Ficedula parva* 12cm

DESCRIPTION Small migrant flycatcher. Like a warbler. Male uniform brown above with greyer head. Throat reddish-orange with grey margins, extending to upper breast. Whitish-

buff below. Female has browner head, and buffish throat and breast. In both, eye dark with pale orbital ring. Tail has wheatear-type pattern, white with dark centre and broad dark terminal band. **VOICE** Sharp *tek* but also more prolonged *terrrrr*. **DISTRIBUTION** In Egypt scarce passage migrant in Delta, Valley, and Sinai. In Region on passage throughout, although largely absent from western and southwestern Arabia. **HABITAT AND HABITS** On passage any area with trees – orchards, plantations, woodland, and oases. Mainly in canopy, where active. When perched often cocks tail, when pattern distinguishes it from other warblers, and flicks wings.

Pied Flycatcher ■ *Ficedula hypoleuca* 13cm

DESCRIPTION Male black and white. Black hood, back, and tail. White throat, breast, and underparts. Small white forehead spot. Wings black, with white patch and narrow white streak at bases of primaries. Female brown above, darker on back and tail. Pale underparts, dusky on breast. Little white on wings, with narrow white streak at bases of primaries. **Collared Flycatcher** *F. albicollis* and **Semi-collared Flycatcher** *F. semitorquata*: males similar but with complete or partial white collars respectively. Females very similar.

VOICE On passage metallic *tek* or sharp *pik*.
DISTRIBUTION In Egypt all three species widespread on passage. In Region Pied and Collared on passage in Levant and northeast Arabia. Semi-collared also to south Arabia and Gulf.
HABITAT AND HABITS On passage any area with trees – orchards, plantations, woodlands, and oases.

Pied Flycatcher   *Collared Flycatcher*

Arabian Babbler ■ *Turdoides squamiceps* 24cm

DESCRIPTION Highly social desert passerine. Slim and long tailed. Pale grey-beige throughout, slightly streaked on back and mantle, and freckled on crown and nape. White throat and pale buff underparts. Long, grey-beige tail. Iris pale (dark in juvenile). Bill strong and slightly downcurved. **VOICE** Chattering, trilling, and piping whistles.
DISTRIBUTION In Egypt confined to south and east Sinai. In Region in southern Levant and Naqab, through much of east and south Arabia and southern Gulf. Similar **Afghan Babbler** *T. huttoni*, browner with warm brown cheeks, has recently colonized Kuwait.

HABITAT AND HABITS Semi-deserts, dry scrub, acacia groves, wadis, and irrigated areas. Highly social in flocks on the ground. Bounds on the ground with tail often cocked and jerked.

Arabian Babbler   *Afghan Babbler*

Nile Valley Sunbird ■ *Hedydipna metallica* 10cm (plus 6cm tail projection in breeding male)

DESCRIPTION Sexes differ. Breeding male iridescent bottle-green above with black breast glossed purple in good light, bright yellow underparts and long, thin tail streamers. Female olive-green above, pale yellow below, with yellow supercilium. Eclipse male similar to female but often with dark on throat. Slender, slightly decurved bill. **VOICE**

Vocal, with variety of high-pitched notes and trills. **DISTRIBUTION** In Region restricted to Nile Valley, where the only sunbird, breeding from Middle Egypt south. Dispersal in winter north to Delta and also east to Red Sea and western Sinai. **HABITAT AND HABITS** Farmland, parks and gardens, and acacia scrub. Nectar feeder attracted to flowering plants and trees. Hotel gardens a good place to look for it. Superficially hummingbird-like but rarely hovers.

Palestine Sunbird ■ *Cinnyris osea* 11cm

DESCRIPTION Sexes differ. Breeding male very dark throughout, appearing black, but in good light glossed blue and purple. Orange pectoral patch rarely visible. Female

greyish throughout, darker above with pale underparts. Eclipse male similar, perhaps with scattered dark feathers. Both sexes short tailed, with slender, downcurved bill. **VOICE** Call sharp *tek*, often repeated, or *tee veet*. Song rather high-pitched trill. **DISTRIBUTION** In Egypt resident in southern and eastern Sinai. Elsewhere resident throughout eastern and southern Arabia, north to Jordan and Levant. **HABITAT AND HABITS** Rocky but well-vegetated wadis, for example Faroun in south Sinai, parks, gardens, and acacia groves in semi-deserts. Ascends to more than 3,000m in mountains. Nectar feeder attracted to flowering shrubs and trees; also insects. Busy and active.

Purple Sunbird ▪ *Cinnyris asiaticus* 10cm

DESCRIPTION Sexes differ. Male similar to Palestine Sunbird (opposite), but no overlap in range. Dark throughout, glossed purple in good light. Female grey-brown above and whitish washed yellow below. Eclipse male as female but with dark on throat and down belly. Both sexes have short tail and slender, downcurved bill. **VOICE** Noisy sunbird. Calls include sharp *chweet* and *dzit*. **DISTRIBUTION** South Asia species extending into Oman, where common around Muscat, and UAE. Similar **Shining Sunbird** *C. habessinicus* (larger with head and mantle glossed green and with scarlet breast-band) found in south and west Arabia and very southeasternmost part of Egypt. **HABITAT AND HABITS** Parks, gardens, mangroves, and agricultural areas. Also thorn scrub and stony deserts. Nectar feeder on flowering shrubs and trees. Active and noisy.

Purple Sunbird

Shining Sunbird

Golden Oriole ▪ *Oriolus oriolus* 24cm

DESCRIPTION Like a thrush in size and form. Male unmistakably brilliant yellow throughout, with black wings, tail, and lores. Female generally greener; pale below, faintly streaked and with yellow largely confined to flanks. In both sexes legs greyish and bill reddish-pink. **VOICE** Call harsh *kraa-ik*. Song rich and mellifluous, like Blackbird's (p. 127). **DISTRIBUTION** In Egypt can be common on passage. Local breeder in parts of northern Arabia and Levant. Elsewhere on passage and occasional in winter. **HABITAT AND HABITS** Gardens, orchards, and wooded areas. On migration even isolated clumps of trees in deserts. Despite brilliant colors, male can be difficult to see in sun-dappled vegetation. Female even more cryptic. Attracted to fruiting trees like mulberry. Flight undulating – note yellow rump.

Isabelline Shrike ■ *Lanius isabellinus* 17cm

(Daurian Shrike)

DESCRIPTION Similar to Red-backed Shrike (below), but paler with bright rufous tail. Male light sandy grey-brown above, with darker flight feathers, and bright rufous rump and tail. Underparts pale, strongly washed buff, and suffused orange on flanks. Dark 'bandit mask'. Female paler, finely scaled below, and with incomplete mask. In flight male shows small white primary patch. **VOICE** Similar to Red-backed's. **DISTRIBUTION** In Egypt scarce passage migrant to north and Sinai. In Region widespread throughout on passage, wintering in southern and eastern Arabia. Race *phoenicuroides* (Turkestan Shrike) summer breeder, Oman. **HABITAT AND HABITS** Open country with trees, acacia scrub, semi-deserts, and arable areas.

Red-backed Shrike ■ *Lanius collurio* 18cm

DESCRIPTION Male has chestnut-brown upperparts and pale grey on nape, crown, and forehead. Black 'bandit mask'. White cheeks and throat, with pale underparts flushed pinkish. Tail black with white flashes. Rump pale grey. Female duller and browner, with brown mask and extensive scaling on underparts. In flight note very little or no white on chestnut/brown wings and pale rump. **VOICE** Song rather scratchy warble. Alarm note repeated *tschek*. **DISTRIBUTION** In Egypt widespread on passage. In Region localized summer breeder in Levant, possibly to Syria. Elsewhere widespread on passage throughout. **HABITAT AND HABITS** Farmland, oases, olive groves, orchards, parks, and scrub. Like other shrikes first-winter birds have paler coloration and extensive scaling.

Great Grey Shrike ■ *Lanius excubitor* 24cm
(Southern Grey Shrike)

DESCRIPTION Main race in Region *L. e. aucheri*. Pale grey mantle, nape, and crown, and black wings and tail. Underparts white with greyish flanks. Black mask with narrow black forehead. Bill stout, dark. In flight note large white patch on primaries, grey rump, and long black tail with white margins. **Lesser Grey Shrike** *L. minor* smaller, suffused pink below and with extensive black forecrown. **VOICE** Song quiet and musical ramble. Calls include harsh *check check*. **DISTRIBUTION** In Egypt common resident throughout Delta, Valley, North Coast, and Sinai,

with some dispersal. In Region resident throughout Levant, south through Arabia and Gulf. **HABITAT AND HABITS** Farmland, groves, scrub, and semi-desert country. Bold, often seen perching in open on wires, prominent branches, and similar.

Great Grey Shrike

Lesser Grey Shrike

Woodchat Shrike ■ *Lanius senator* 18cm

DESCRIPTION Shorter-tailed than Masked Shrike (p. 146). Male black and white with bright chestnut crown and nape. Black 'bandit mask', extending well on to forehead; white throat and underparts. Back and wings black with bold white 'shoulder' patch. Whitish to grey rump and black tail with white margins. Female similar but slightly paler, with

pale buff at bill-base. In flight variable white on primaries. **VOICE** Song loud and streaming. Calls include *chak chak* and hoarse trill. **DISTRIBUTION** In Egypt widespread throughout on passage. In Region summer breeder in Levant and widespread on passage throughout. Rare in winter in southern Arabia. **HABITAT AND HABITS** Farmland, oases, olive groves, orchards, parks, and scrub. Similar to Masked but note pale rump and chestnut crown.

Masked Shrike ■ *Lanius nubicus* 18cm

DESCRIPTION Small, long-tailed shrike. Adult male black on rump, back, mantle, nape, and crown. Wings black and white, including bold white 'shoulders'. Underparts white flushed deep orange on flanks. Forehead white extending over eye, and with black 'bandit mask' separating from white cheeks and throat. Long tail black with white margins. Female similar but paler throughout. In flight shows black wings with white primary patch. **VOICE** Song similar to those of some warblers. Calls include harsh *krrrrrr*. **DISTRIBUTION** In

Egypt fairly common on passage throughout, especially east and Sinai. Summer breeder in Levant south to Jordan. On passage throughout with a few wintering in south Arabia. **HABITAT AND HABITS** Light woodland, farmland, olive groves, orchards, and scrub. Often pumps long tail up and down.

House Crow ■ *Corvus splendens* 43cm WS 76cm

(Indian House Crow)

DESCRIPTION Rather dapper, slim crow. Largely black with grey (generally darker grey than in larger Hooded Crow, opposite) on nape, neck, and breast. Extent of grey varies. Proportionately longer billed than Hooded, with steep forehead and domed head giving different profile. On ground long legged. Legs and feet dark. **VOICE** Can be noisy, especially in large groups. Incessant *waah waah* or *krrah* like Hooded's, but higher. **DISTRIBUTION** In and around ports and human settlements along all coasts of Arabia. Also introduced in Egypt in Suez, and expanding range along Red Sea coasts. **HABITAT AND HABITS** Noisy and aggressive; increasing in numbers throughout Region. Gregarious, often in noisy flocks, especially at roosts.

Hooded Crow ■ *Corvus cornix* 47cm WS 94cm
(Carrion Crow)

DESCRIPTION Archetypal grey and black crow. Black with grey mantle, nape, and underparts. Black throat extends down centre of breast. Stout black bill. Black legs and feet. In flight note grey underwing-coverts. **VOICE** Noisy, with harsh, grating *krrah krrah*, often repeated. **DISTRIBUTION** In Egypt very common resident throughout Delta and Valley, parts of North Coast, and Sinai. Also Western Oases. Elsewhere Levant and western Jordan. Largely absent from Arabia. **HABITAT AND HABITS** Common, even ubiquitous, in cities, towns, and villages. Also agricultural areas and open land with trees, but absent from deserts, where replaced by Brown-necked Raven (below). Opportunistic and omnivorous.

Brown-necked Raven ■ *Corvus ruficollis* 50cm WS 110cm

DESCRIPTION Common all-black crow of semi-desert and desert regions. Black throughout. 'Brown neck' only seen as bronzy-brown gloss on nape in good light. Bill quite long. In flight all black below with longish, slightly wedge-shaped tail. **VOICE** Call similar to Hooded Crow's (above), *kree-eh*. **DISTRIBUTION** In Egypt common crow of desert and semi-desert areas, including Sinai, where it replaces Hooded. Elsewhere throughout Region, including eastern Jordan but absent from northern Levant. **HABITAT AND HABITS** Deserts and semi-deserts, including plains and wadis. Replaced in mountainous areas of eastern Arabia, and locally north to Jordan (Petra) by **Fan-tailed Raven** C. *rhipidurus*, also all black but with heavier bill and very short tail almost continuous with broad wings in flight.

Brown-necked Raven

Fan-tailed Raven

Common Myna ■ *Acridotheres tristis* 23cm

DESCRIPTION Noisy, sociable myna. Dark maroon-brown; slightly paler below with striking white patch on wing. Head darker, almost blackish, with bare yellow skin around eye. White vent. Tail blackish with white outer tips. Bill yellow. Legs yellow. In flight note white patch on primaries. **VOICE** Very vocal, with loud, strident song. Alarm call rendered as harsh *traaah*. **DISTRIBUTION** In Egypt recent colonist, possibly from Saudi populations recorded on Red Sea coast and elsewhere. Established populations in western Arabia, especially around Jeddah, and much of Gulf to eastern Oman. **HABITAT AND HABITS** Urban centres, ports, villages, parks, gardens, and wasteland. Loud and obvious, often occurring in flocks. Walks stiffly and erect.

Tristram's Starling ■ *Onychognathus tristramii* 25cm

(Tristram's Grackle)

DESCRIPTION Distinctive, all-dark starling. Slim and long tailed. Male glossy blue-black throughout with bright chestnut patch on wing. Female entirely blackish-brown with grey head and chestnut wing-patch. Bill and legs black. In flight, chestnut wing-patch with black trailing edge striking. **VOICE** Very loud and vocal. Calls like tuning a shortwave radio, loud, weird whistles that are amplified by mountains. **DISTRIBUTION** In Egypt resident, confined to mountains of south Sinai, especially around St Katherine's. In Region resident from Naqab to mountains of western and southern Arabia. **HABITAT AND HABITS** Mountains, ravines and gorges, semi-deserts, and also towns and villages. Flocks noisy and active, often feeding in orchards and gardens, and nesting in rock cavities or on buildings – even in central Sanaa.

House Sparrow ■ *Passer domesticus* 15cm

DESCRIPTION Archetypal 'small brown bird'. Male heavily streaked brown above; grey crown with chestnut sides and nape. Black lores, throat, and upper breast; extent of black variable with age and status. Dusky-greyish cheeks and plain pale grey underparts. White wing-bar. Female has plainer head, largely dull grey-brown with paler supercilium and pale throat. Duller wing-bar. Bill stout but pointed. **VOICE** Variety of chirps and cheeps. Can be very loud at evening roost. **DISTRIBUTION** In Egypt very common resident throughout, including in isolated oases. In Region widespread common resident throughout, with exception of south-central Arabia. **HABITATS AND HABITS** Commensal. Cities, towns, and villages; also farmland and waste ground. Social, occurring in flocks and roosting in large congregations. Nests on buildings; often semi-colonial.

Spanish Sparrow ■ *Passer hispaniolensis* 15cm

DESCRIPTION Male has back streaked blackish and brown wings with white wing-bar. Differs from male House Sparrow (above) by completely chestnut crown, white cheeks, and narrow white supercilium. Black lores and throat extend in bold streaks on to breast and flanks. Female very similar to female House, but sometimes with subtle streaking on underparts. Bill stocky but pointed. **VOICE** Variety of chirps and cheeps. **DISTRIBUTION** In Egypt fairly common winter visitor to north, including Sinai and Western Oases. In Region resident in Levant south to Naqab and also Gulf. More widespread in winter. **HABITAT AND HABITS** Less urban than House. Towns, villages, groves, plantations, and more open farmland. Often in flocks and nests semi-colonially.

Dead Sea Sparrow ■ *Passer moabiticus* 13cm

DESCRIPTION Small local sparrow. Male has streaked brown back and chestnut wing-coverts. Grey head with pale supercilium turning buff behind eye. Grey cheeks and

black throat with yellow sides. Underparts pale greyish. Female like small, pale House Sparrow (p. 149), but with dark spots on undertail-coverts. May show yellow tinge on neck. Compact bill. **VOICE** As House but weaker. **DISTRIBUTION** Rare winter visitor to Sinai. Local resident in Syria, and southern Levant through Naqab. Some dispersal in winter. **HABITAT AND HABITS** Thick scrub and tamarisk clumps, often near water. Somewhat nomadic in winter, moving to agricultural areas but not as tied to humans as Region's other sparrows.

Pale Rock Sparrow ■ *Carpospiza brachydactyla* 15cm
(Pale Rockfinch)

DESCRIPTION Nondescript, plain sparrow. Unstreaked pale grey-brown throughout, with white panel on wings and narrow white wing-bar. Head pale brown with whitish supercilium and malar stripe, darker cheeks, and dark eye. Throat and belly whitish; breast more buff.

Bill pale, heavy, and with curved culmen. In flight note short dark tail with white tips, and long, pointed wings. **VOICE** Song buzzing *tsse tsse tsseeeeee*, likened to insect. **DISTRIBUTION** In Egypt uncommon on passage to Sinai and Eastern Desert. Very local and patchy summer breeder in Levant, and north Arabia and Oman. Widespread on passage with a few in winter. **HABITAT AND HABITS** Rocky scrub, hillsides, and semi-deserts; in winter in cultivation. In flocks on passage. Feeds on the ground, where appears rather lark-like.

Streaked Weaver ■ *Ploceus manyar* 14cm

DESCRIPTION Sparrow-like weaver of damp habitat. Male grey-brown above heavily streaked dark. Head dark with blackish cheeks and throat, and bright yellow forehead and crown. Underparts strongly streaked. Heavy bill dark and pointed. Female has streaked head with yellowish supercilium and moustachial stripe, and dark malar stripe. Throat whitish. Bill pinkish-grey. **VOICE** Meandering, jumbled song. Call short *chirt*. **DISTRIBUTION** In Egypt introduced, established resident in Delta from Cairo north. May be spreading.

In Region introduced, established populations in Gulf and eastern Arabia. Look out for escaped **Village Weaver** *P. cucullatus* and **Lesser Masked Weaver** (race indeterminate) both also with established populations in Gulf; both much yellower. **HABITATS AND HABITS** Moist habitats, wetlands, reedbeds, and water margins with dank vegetation. Nest woven among reed stems.

Streaked Weaver   *Lesser Masked Weaver*

Indian Silverbill ■ *Lonchura malabarica* 11cm

DESCRIPTION Small, slim, heavy-billed finch. Unbarred beige-brown above with black primaries. Pale cream below including throat. Tail black and pointed. Rump and vent bright white. Bill large, conical, and silver and black. Very similar **African Silverbill** *L. cantans* has subtle barring on wings and black rump. **VOICE** Various *cheets* and *tchwits*. Trilling song. **DISTRIBUTION** Introduced in Egypt. Now in Cairo, Delta and expanding, for example to Fayoum, Sinai.

In Region introduced in Naqab and pockets of eastern Arabia. Native and introduced in Oman north through Gulf – expanding west. African native in extreme southeastern Egypt and southwestern Arabia. **HABITAT AND HABITS** Hills, wadis, farmland, plantations, groves, parks, and gardens. Often in small, vocal flocks. Diagnostic white rump very clear in flight and at rest.

Indian Silverbill   *African Silverbill*

Red Avadavat ■ *Amandava amandava* 10cm

DESCRIPTION Tiny, red-billed finch. Breeding male bright red throughout, darker and browner on wings. Wings have white spots. Below red, spotted with white. Female has grey

brown upperparts; yellow-beige below. Winter male as female but greyer. Both sexes have bright crimson rump and rounded black tail. Bill stubby and bright red. **VOICE** Call high-pitched twittering, constant in flocks. **DISTRIBUTION** In Egypt introduced to Delta and Valley, where common established resident. In Region introduced, with local populations in Saudi and Gulf. **HABITAT AND HABITS** Farmland, and damp scrub, reedbeds, irrigation canals, and similar. Often in small, vocal flocks – note tiny size and red bill.

Serin ■ *Serinus serinus* 12cm
(European Serin)

DESCRIPTION Small, compact finch. Male olive, streaked dark above. Yellow head with darker crown and cheeks. Yellow throat and breast with white belly and streaked flanks. Female similar but with much less yellow. Bill tiny, stubby. In flight narrow yellow wing-bars, dark, forked tail, and yellow rump. **VOICE** Song very rapid jingle, often from exposed branch or tree-top. Call metallic *zrrlt*. **DISTRIBUTION** In Egypt local breeder confined to northeastern Sinai. Local breeder in northwestern Syria and southern Levant, with winter dispersal south to northern Arabia. **HABITAT AND HABITS** Orchards, plantations, parks, and gardens. Also more open country in winter. Small size and tiny bill distinctive, as is loud song from prominent perch. Flight fast and undulating.

Adult

Juvenile

Syrian Serin ■ *Serinus syriacus* 13cm

DESCRIPTION Like Serin (opposite), but slightly larger and longer tailed. Male olive-grey above, subtly streaked on mantle, and yellow-green on wings. Crown grey, with deep yellow forehead and around eye; yellow throat. Underparts pale grey-yellow, with grey flanks and pale vent. Female greyer with much less yellow. Stubby dark bill. In flight note yellow rump, tail-sides, and secondary coverts. **VOICE** Soft, twittering song. Calls include sharp *cheep*, sometimes repeated, and *tseer*. **DISTRIBUTION** Endemic to Region. Rare winter visitor to Egypt in Sinai. Local resident breeder in western Levant north to Syria, with some dispersal in winter. **HABITAT AND HABITS** Breeds in broadleaved and coniferous wooded mountains and hillsides. In winter often in flocks in more open country, feeding on the ground.

Greenfinch ■ *Carduelis chloris* 15cm
(European Greenfinch)

DESCRIPTION Thickset, dull green finch. Male largely olive-green, yellower below and with bright yellow edges to primaries and tail. Tail otherwise forked and with dark terminal band. Head has dark lores and grey ear-coverts. Female duller and greyer, with less yellow.

Bill pale pinkish and pointed. In flight note yellow on wings and tail. **VOICE** Song either wheezy and repetitive, or more musical. Calls include abrupt *chupp*. **DISTRIBUTION** In Egypt fairly common resident in Delta and north Sinai. More widespread in winter across North Coast. In Region resident in western Levant, with some dispersal south and east in winter. **HABITAT AND HABITS** Breeds in woodland, parks, gardens, and orchards. In winter often in flocks in more open country, including farmland, rough scrub, and wasteland.

Goldfinch ■ *Carduelis carduelis* 13cm
(European Goldfinch)

DESCRIPTION Small finch. Pale beige-brown; whiter below. Head has bright red facial mask; black on crown down to and around back of neck. Contrasting white ear-coverts, cheeks, and throat. Wings black with bright yellow panel. Bill whitish and pointed. In flight wings black and yellow. Rump white. **VOICE** Quiet, trilling song. Calls include *litt*,

de-litt or *de-litt-dits*, often from feeding flocks. **DISTRIBUTION** In Egypt common resident in Delta, northern Valley, and across North Coast, including Sinai. More widespread in winter. In Region resident in western Levant and locally north Arabia, with winter dispersal south and east. **HABITAT AND HABITS** Agricultural areas, wooded hillsides, and plantations. In winter in more open country. In winter often in flocks ('charms'). Attracted to seeding thistles, sunflowers, and similar.

Sinai Rosefinch ■ *Carpodacus synoicus* 14cm

DESCRIPTION Male bright rose-pink with streaked brown mantle and brown wings. Face and throat deeper cherry-pink, with 'frosting' on forehead and crown. Paler pink towards belly and pale vent. Pink rump. Forked brown tail. Female plain brown and featureless; paler below. **Common Rosefinch** C. *erythrinus*, uncommon passage migrant, deeper red on head and breast in male. **DISTRIBUTION** In Egypt resident, confined to mountains of south Sinai, for example around St Katherine's. In Region resident in Naqab south to northeastern Arabia. **HABITAT AND HABITS** Barren, rocky mountains, gorges, and ravines, but also gardens and orchards in these areas. Unobtrusive despite male's colors. Easily seen at sites such as St Katherine's or Petra in Jordan.

Sinai Rosefinch

Common Rosefinch

Trumpeter Finch ■ *Bucanetes githagineus* 14cm

DESCRIPTION Similar to Sinai Rosefinch (p. 155). Breeding male compact; grey-brown above with pink on wings. Underparts pale, washed pink. Head greyish, tinged pink on forehead and throat. Rump pink. Bill bright reddish-orange. Female and winter male

pale grey-beige, sometimes tinged pink, with pale rump and pale pink bill. Legs reddish-pink. In flight note pinkish rump. **VOICE** Supposedly like child's trumpet; wheezy *cheeee*. Call shorter *chee* or *chit*. **DISTRIBUTION** Nomadic. In Egypt fairly common resident in Eastern Desert, north to east of Cairo and Sinai. In Region through much of Levant, south through much of Arabia, more locally in Gulf. **HABITAT AND HABITS** Barren, rocky hillsides, wadis, dry plains, and semi-deserts. Often feeds on the ground in small, vocal flocks.

Striolated Bunting ■ *Emberiza striolata* 14cm

DESCRIPTION Bunting of remote, rocky habitat. Male has lightly streaked brown upperparts. Underparts with lightly streaked, greyish breast shade into rufous lower breast and paler belly. Head has streaked grey crown and throat, white supercilium, black eye-stripe, and black and white striped cheeks. Female similar but drabber. In flight shows buff margins to dark tail. Bill pointed, with yellowish lower mandible. **VOICE** Song short, simple melody. Calls include *swee-doo*. **DISTRIBUTION** In Egypt resident, confined to

south Sinai. In Region found from Naqab and Sinai border, through much of Arabia to Oman and southern Gulf. **HABITAT AND HABITS** Barren, rocky mountains, often with scanty vegetation, wadis, and oases. Previously lumped with extralimital **House Bunting** *E. sahari.*

Ortolan Bunting ▪ *Emberiza hortulana* 16cm

DESCRIPTION Slim, pastel-colored bunting. Male tawny-brown above with bold dark streaks, dark tail, and streaked, dull brown rump. Underparts uniform orange-brown. Head, neck, and upper breast greenish-grey. Throat and moustachial stripe yellow. Pale eye-ring. Bill rather long, pointed, and pinkish. Legs pinkish. Female similar but with thin dark streaking on head and breast. **VOICE** Call low *sle-ee* or short *plett*. **DISTRIBUTION** In Egypt widespread on passage. Local summer breeder in central Levant and on passage throughout. Winters in tropical Africa. **HABITAT AND HABITS** Open scrubland, groves, and woodland glades. On passage also desert margins and oases. Often in flocks feeding on the ground. Nocturnal migrant.

Cretzschmar's Bunting ▪ *Emberiza caesia* 15cm

DESCRIPTION Similar to but slightly smaller than Ortolan Bunting (above). Male tawny-brown above with bold dark streaks, dark tail, and streaked tawny-brown rump. Underparts uniform rust-brown. Head, neck, and upper breast blue-grey. Throat and moustachial stripe brick-red. Pale eye-ring. Bill fairly long, pointed, and pinkish. Legs pinkish. Female similar but with thin, dark streaking on head and breast, and pale throat. **VOICE** Calls include *tsrip* and *plett*. **DISTRIBUTION** In Egypt on passage through Valley east to Sinai. In Region breeds down eastern Levant and Naqab. On passage through Levant to eastern Arabia. **HABITAT AND HABITS** Open scrubland, groves, and rocky slopes. On passage often coastal; also desert margins and oases. Often in flocks feeding on the ground. Nocturnal migrant.

Black-headed Bunting ■ *Emberiza melanocephala* 16cm

DESCRIPTION Slim, long-tailed bunting. Breeding male unmistakable. Upperparts with unstreaked, reddish-brown mantle extending to rump. Underparts yellow. Head has black hood, yellow throat, and incomplete collar. Bill rather heavy and grey. Legs dark pink. Female has duller brown upperparts and rump, paler yellow underparts, and streaked grey hood. **VOICE** Calls include *choop* and harsher *zrit*. Song similar to Common Whitethroat's (p. 136). **DISTRIBUTION** In Egypt scarce on passage, mainly in Sinai. In Region summer breeder in western Levant south to Sinai border. On passage in northern and eastern Arabia and Gulf. **HABITAT AND HABITS** Open country, including upland slopes with bushes, farmland, groves, and orchards. Sadly, appears in bird markets in Gulf.

Corn Bunting ■ *Emberiza calandra* 18cm

DESCRIPTION Large, streaky brown bunting. Dark, heavily streaked grey-brown above. Below whitish-buff streaked dark on breast and flanks. Rump and tail brown. Head looks large, with dark malar stripe and throat margins, and dark spot on ear-coverts. Bill robust and yellowish-pink. Legs pinkish. In flight note absence of any white on tail, rump, or wings. **VOICE** Call sharp *tritt*. Song often likened to jangling keys. **DISTRIBUTION** In Egypt fairly common winter visitor to North Coast, Delta, and Sinai. In Region resident in Levant and very locally in eastern Arabia. Winter and on passage over much of Region except southwestern Arabia. **HABITAT AND HABITS** Farmland, scrub, and pasture. In flight often shows dangling legs and feet.

As the total species count for the whole of Egypt and the Middle East is high, the checklist below covers all the birds of Egypt and their status in the country. These species are also found in the Region as described in the text. For checklists of every bird ever recorded in the Region, go to 'OSME Region List ORL'. The English names are based on the International Ornithological Congress (IOC) World Bird Names: www.worldbirdnames. org/names.html. The systematics are based on the Association of European Records and Rarities Committees (AERC) TAC Western Palearctic list: www.aerc.eu/tac.html.

Categories
A   Wild origin, seen after 1950 (444 species)
B   Wild origin, seen before 1950 but not after (9 species)
C   Introduced with self-sustainable populations or originating from established populations in another country (6 species)
GE   Observed in Gebel Elba only (7 species)

Status Abbreviations
The status of each bird is according to Goodman and Meininger's *The Birds of Egypt* 1989 on which the official checklist is based. The IUCN status uses the official IUCN Red List Status. The abbreviations are as follows:
CB   Casual breeder
FB   Former breeder
IB   Introduced breeder
MB   Migrant breeder
RB   Resident breeder
AV   Accidental visitor or vagrant
PV   Passage visitor
WV   Winter visitor
( )   Abbreviation in parentheses indicates that the status is variable or erratic e.g (PV) means an 'irregular passage visitor'
?   Status uncertain

IUCN abbreviations
LC   Least Concern
NT   Near Threatened
VU   Vulnerable
EN   Endangered
CR   Critically Endangered

Common name	Scientific name	Category	Status	IUCN
Struthionidae (Ostriches)				
Ostrich	*Struthio camelus*	A	RB?	LC
Anatidae (Ducks and Geese)				
Mute Swan	*Cygnus olor*	A	(WV)	LC
Whooper Swan	*Cygnus cygnus*	A	AV	LC
Bean Goose	*Anser fabalis*	A	AV	LC
Greater White-fronted Goose	*Anser albifrons*	A	(WV)	LC
Lesser White-fronted Goose	*Anser erythropus*	A	AV	VU

Common name	Scientific name	Category	Status	IUCN
Greylag Goose	Anser anser	B	AV	LC
Barnacle Goose	Branta leucopsis	B	AV	LC
Brant Goose	Branta bernicla	B	AV	LC
Red-breasted Goose	Branta ruficollis	B	AV	NT/VU
Egyptian Goose	Alopochen aegyptiaca	A	RB	LC
Ruddy Shelduck	Tadorna ferruginea	A	PV WV	LC
Common Shelduck	Tadorna tadorna	A	WV	LC
Eurasian Wigeon	Anas penelope	A	PV WV	LC
Gadwall	Anas strepera	A	PV WV	LC
Eurasian Teal	Anas crecca	A	PV WV	LC
Mallard	Anas platyrhynchos	A	CB PV WV	LC
Northern Pintail	Anas acuta	A	PV WV	LC
Garganey	Anas querquedula	A	PV	LC
Blue-winged Teal	Anas discors	A	AV	LC
Northern Shoveler	Anas clypeata	A	PV WV	LC
Marbled Duck	Marmaronetta angustirostris	A	RB? (WV)	VU
Red-crested Pochard	Netta rufina	A	WV	LC
Common Pochard	Aythya ferina	A	PV WV	LC
Ferruginous Duck	Aythya nyroca	A	PV WV	NT/LC
Tufted Duck	Aythya fuligula	A	PV WV	LC
Velvet Scoter	Melanitta fusca	A	AV	VU
Smew	Mergellus albellus	A	(WV)	LC
Red-breasted Merganser	Mergus serrator	A	(WV)	LC
White-headed Duck	Oxyura leucocephala	A	(WV)	EN
Phasianidae (Pheasants, Partridges and Grouse)				
Chukar Partridge	Alectoris chukar	A	RB	LC
Barbary Partridge	Alectoris barbara	A	RB?	LC
Sand Partridge	Ammoperdix heyi	A	RB	LC
Common Quail	Coturnix coturnix	A	(RB) PV WV	LC
Podicipedidae (Grebes)				
Little Grebe	Tachybaptus ruficollis	A	RB WV	LC
Great Crested Grebe	Podiceps cristatus	A	FB WV	LC
Red-necked Grebe	Podiceps grisegena	A	AV	LC
Black-necked Grebe	Podiceps nigricollis	A	WV	LC
Diomedeidae (Albatrosses)				
Shy Albatross	Thalassarche cauta	A	AV	NT
Procellariidae (Shearwaters)				
Cory's Shearwater	Calonectris diomedea	A	PV WV	LC
Streaked Shearwater	Calonectris leucomelas	A	AV	LC
Sooty Shearwater	Puffinus griseus	A	PV	LC
Yelkouan Shearwater	Puffinus yelkouan	A	PV WV	LC
Balearic Shearwater	Puffinus mauretanicus	A	AV	LC
Hydrobatidae (Storm Petrels)				
Wilson's Storm Petrel	Oceanites oceanicus	A	PV	LC
Leach's Storm Petrel	Oceanodroma leucorhoa	A	AV	VU
Phaethontidae (Tropicbirds)				
Red-billed Tropicbird	Phaethon aethereus	A	RB	LC
Sulidae (Gannets and Boobies)				
Brown Booby	Sula leucogaster	A	RB	LC
Northern Gannet	Morus bassanus	A	PV WV	LC
Phalacrocoracidae (Cormorants and Shags)				
Great Cormorant	Phalacrocorax carbo	A	PV WV	LC
European Shag	Phalacrocorax aristotelis	A	AV	LC

Common name	Scientific name	Category	Status	IUCN
Reed Cormorant	*Phalacrocorax africanus*	A	FB	LC
Family Anhingidae (Darters)				
Darter	*Anhinga melanogaster*	A	AV	NT
Pelecanidae (Pelicans)				
Great White Pelican	*Pelecanus onocrotalus*	A	PV WV	LC
Dalmatian Pelican	*Pelecanus crispus*	A	WV	VU
Pink-backed Pelican	*Pelecanus rufescens*	A	PV	LC
Ardeidae (Herons, Egrets and Bitterns)				
Eurasian Bittern	*Botaurus stellaris*	A	WV	LC
Little Bittern	*Ixobrychus minutus*	A	RB PV WV	LC
Yellow Bittern	*Ixobrychus sinensis*	A	RB?	LC
Black-crowned Night Heron	*Nycticorax nycticorax*	A	RB? PV WV	LC
Striated Heron	*Butorides striata*	A	RB PV	LC
Squacco Heron	*Ardeola ralloides*	A	RB PV WV	LC
Cattle Egret	*Bubulcus ibis*	A	RB PV WV	LC
Western Reef Heron	*Egretta gularis*	A	RB	LC
Little Egret	*Egretta garzetta*	A	RB PV WV	LC
Great Egret	*Egretta alba*	A	PV WV	LC
Grey Heron	*Ardea cinerea*	A	CB PV WV	LC
Purple Heron	*Ardea purpurea*	A	PV WV	LC
Goliath Heron	*Ardea goliath*	A	RB PV	LC
Ciconiidae (Storks)				
Yellow-billed Stork	*Mycteria ibis*	A	(PV)	LC
African Openbill	*Anastomus lamelligerus*	A	AV	LC
Black Stork	*Ciconia nigra*	A	PV (WV)	LC
White Stork	*Ciconia ciconia*	A	PV (WV)	LC
Threskionidae (Ibises and Spoonbills)				
Glossy Ibis	*Plegadis falcinellus*	A	PV (WV)	LC
Sacred Ibis	*Threskiornis aethiopicus*	B	FB	LC
Eurasian Spoonbill	*Platalea leucorodia*	A	RB PV WV	LC
Phoenicopteridae (Flamingos)				
Greater Flamingo	*Phoenicopterus roseus*	A	RB PV WV	LC
Lesser Flamingo	*Phoenicopterus minor*	A	AV	NT
Accipitridae (Birds of Prey)				
European Honey Buzzard	*Pernis apivorus*	A	PV	LC
Crested Honey Buzzard	*Pernis ptilorhynchus*	A	PV?	LC
Black-winged Kite	*Elanus caeruleus*	A	RB	LC
Black Kite	*Milvus migrans*	A	RB PV WV	LC
Red Kite	*Milvus milvus*	A	(PV)	LC
African Fish Eagle	*Haliaeetus vocifer*	A	AV	LC
White-tailed Eagle	*Haliaeetus albicilla*	A	FB? (WV)	LC
Bearded Vulture	*Gypaetus barbatus*	A	RB (WV)	LC
Egyptian Vulture	*Neophron percnopterus*	A	RB PV (WV)	EN
White-backed Vulture	*Gyps africanus*	A	AV	CR
Griffon Vulture	*Gyps fulvus*	A	FB PV (WV)	LC
Rüppell's Vulture	*Gyps rueppellii*	A	(PV)	CR
Lappet-faced Vulture	*Torgos tracheliotus*	A	RB	EN
Cinereous Vulture	*Aegypius monachus*	A	(PV) (WV)	NT
Short-toed Snake Eagle	*Circaetus gallicus*	A	CB PV (WV)	LC
Bateleur	*Terathopius ecaudatus*	A	RB?	EN
Western Marsh Harrier	*Circus aeruginosus*	A	PV WV	LC
Northern Harrier	*Circus cyaneus*	A	PV WV	LC
Pallid Harrier	*Circus macrourus*	A	PV WV	NT

Common name	Scientific name	Category	Status	IUCN
Montagu's Harrier	*Circus pygargus*	A	PV (WV)	LC
Gabar Goshawk	*Micronisus gabar*	B	AV	LC
Northern Goshawk	*Accipiter gentilis*	A	WV	LC
Eurasian Sparrowhawk	*Accipiter nisus*	A	PV WV	LC
Levant Sparrowhawk	*Accipiter brevipes*	A	PV	LC
Common Buzzard	*Buteo buteo*	A	PV WV	LC
Long-legged Buzzard	*Buteo rufinus*	A	CB PV WV	LC
Lesser Spotted Eagle	*Aquila pomarina*	A	PV (WV)	LC
Greater Spotted Eagle	*Aquila clanga*	A	PV WV	VU
Tawny Eagle	*Aquila rapax*	A	AV	LC
Steppe Eagle	*Aquila nipalensis*	A	PV (WV)	LC
Eastern Imperial Eagle	*Aquila heliaca*	A	PV (WV)	VU
Golden Eagle	*Aquila chrysaetos*	A	RB (WV)	LC
Verreaux's Eagle	*Aquila verreauxii*	A	RB	LC
Wahlberg's Eagle	*Aquila wahlbergi*	A	AV	LC
Booted Eagle	*Aquila pennata*	A	PV (WV)	LC
Bonelli's Eagle	*Aquila fasciata*	A	RB PV WV	LC
Pandionidae (Ospreys)				
Osprey	*Pandion haliaetus*	A	RB PV WV	LC
Falconidae (Falcons)				
Lesser Kestrel	*Falco naumanni*	A	CB PV (WV)	LC
Common Kestrel	*Falco tinnunculus*	A	RB PV WV	LC
Red-footed Falcon	*Falco vespertinus*	A	PV (WV)	LC
Merlin	*Falco columbarius*	A	WV	LC
Eurasian Hobby	*Falco subbuteo*	A	MB PV (WV)	LC
Eleonora's Falcon	*Falco eleonorae*	A	PV	LC
Sooty Falcon	*Falco concolor*	A	MB (WV)	LC
Lanner Falcon	*Falco biarmicus*	A	RB WV	LC
Saker Falcon	*Falco cherrug*	A	PV WV	EN
Peregrine Falcon	*Falco peregrinus*	A	PV WV	LC
Barbary Falcon	*Falco pelegrinoides*	A	RB PV?	LC
Rallidae (Rails and Crakes)				
Water Rail	*Rallus aquaticus*	A	RB WV	LC
Spotted Crake	*Porzana porzana*	A	PV WV	LC
Little Crake	*Porzana parva*	A	CB? PV WV	LC
Baillon's Crake	*Porzana pusilla*	A	RB PV WV	LC
Corn Crake	*Crex crex*	A	PV	LC
Common Moorhen	*Gallinula chloropus*	A	RB PV WV	LC
Purple Swamphen	*Porphyrio porphyrio*	A	RB	LC
Eurasian Coot	*Fulica atra*	A	RB WV	LC
Gruidae (Cranes)				
Common Crane	*Grus grus*	A	PV (WV)	LC
Demoiselle Crane	*Grus virgo*	A	PV (WV)	LC
Otididae (Bustards)				
Little Bustard	*Tetrax tetrax*	A	(WV)	NT
Houbara Bustard	*Chlamydotis undulata*	A	RB (WV)	VU
Macqueen's Bustard	*Chlamydotis macqueenii*	A	RB (WV)	VU
Great Bustard	*Otis tarda*	A	AV	VU
Rostratulidae (Painted Snipes)				
Greater Painted Snipe	*Rostratula benghalensis*	A	RB	LC
Haematopodidae (Oystercatchers)				
Eurasian Oystercatcher	*Haematopus ostralegus*	A	PV WV	LC

Common name	Scientific name	Category	Status	IUCN
Recurvirostridae (Avocets and Stilts)				
Black-winged Stilt	Himantopus himantopus	A	MB PV WV	LC
Pied Avocet	Recurvirostra avosetta	A	CB PV WV	LC
Dromadidae (Crab Plover)				
Crab Plover	Dromas ardeola	A	WV PV	LC
Burhinidae (Thick-knees)				
Eurasian Stone-curlew	Burhinus oedicnemus	A	RB PV WV	LC
Senegal Thick-knee	Burhinus senegalensis	A	RB	LC
Glareolidae (Coursers and Pratincoles)				
Egyptian Plover	Pluvianus aegyptius	B	FB AV?	LC
Cream-colored Courser	Cursorius cursor	A	RB PV WV	LC
Collared Pratincole	Glareola pratincola	A	MB PV (WV)	LC
Black-winged Pratincole	Glareola nordmanni	A	PV	LC
Charadriidae (Plovers)				
Little Ringed Plover	Charadrius dubius	A	(MB) PV WV	LC
Common Ringed Plover	Charadrius hiaticula	A	PV WV	LC
Kittlitz's Plover	Charadrius pecuarius	A	RB	LC
Three-banded Plover	Charadrius tricollaris	A	AV	LC
Kentish Plover	Charadrius alexandrinus	A	RB PV WV	LC
Lesser Sand Plover	Charadrius mongolus	A	PV	LC
Greater Sand Plover	Charadrius leschenaultii	A	PV WV CB?	LC
Caspian Plover	Charadrius asiaticus	A	PV	LC
Eurasian Dotterel	Charadrius morinellus	A	WV	LC
European Golden Plover	Pluvialis apricaria	A	PV WV	LC
Grey Plover	Pluvialis squatarola	A	PV WV	LC
Spur-winged Lapwing	Vanellus spinosus	A	RB PV WV	LC
Sociable Lapwing	Vanellus gregarius	A	PV (WV)	CR
White-tailed Lapwing	Vanellus leucurus	A	PV (WV)	LC
Northern Lapwing	Vanellus vanellus	A	PV WV	LC
Scolopacidae (Sandpipers)				
Red Knot	Calidris canutus	A	(PV)	LC
Sanderling	Calidris alba	A	PV WV	LC
Little Stint	Calidris minuta	A	PV WV	LC
Temminck's Stint	Calidris temminckii	A	PV WV	LC
Pectoral Sandpiper	Calidris melanotos	A	AV	LC
Curlew Sandpiper	Calidris ferruginea	A	PV (WV)	LC
Dunlin	Calidris alpina	A	PV WV	LC
Broad-billed Sandpiper	Limicola falcinellus	A	PV (WV)	LC
Ruff	Philomachus pugnax	A	PV WV	LC
Jack Snipe	Lymnocryptes minimus	A	PV WV	LC
Common Snipe	Gallinago gallinago	A	PV WV	LC
Great Snipe	Gallinago media	A	PV (WV)	LC
Pin-tailed/Swinhoe's Snipe	Gallinago stenura/megala	A	AV	LC
Eurasian Woodcock	Scolopax rusticola	A	WV	LC
Black-tailed Godwit	Limosa limosa	A	PV WV	NT
Bar-tailed Godwit	Limosa lapponica	A	PV WV	LC
Whimbrel	Numenius phaeopus	A	PV (WV)	LC
Slender-billed Curlew	Numenius tenuirostris	A	(PV) (WV)?	CR
Eurasian Curlew	Numenius arquata	A	PV WV	LC
Terek Sandpiper	Xenus cinereus	A	PV	LC
Common Sandpiper	Actitis hypoleucos	A	PV WV	LC
Green Sandpiper	Tringa ochropus	A	PV WV	LC
Spotted Redshank	Tringa erythropus	A	PV WV	LC

Common name	Scientific name	Category	Status	IUCN
Common Greenshank	Tringa nebularia	A	Pv WV	LC
Marsh Sandpiper	Tringa stagnatilis	A	PV WV	LC
Wood Sandpiper	Tringa glareola	A	PV WV	LC
Common Redshank	Tringa totanus	A	PV WV	LC
Ruddy Turnstone	Arenaria interpres	A	PV WV	LC
Red-necked Phalarope	Phalaropus lobatus	A	PV	LC
Red Phalarope	Phalaropus fulicarius	A	(PV) (WV)	LC
Stercorariidae (Skuas)				
Pomarine Skua	Stercorarius pomarinus	A	PV WV	LC
Parasitic Jaeger	Stercorarius parasiticus	A	PV WV	LC
Long-tailed Jaeger	Stercorarius longicaudus	A	(PV)	LC
Laridae (Gulls)				
Sooty Gull	Larus hemprichii	A	RB	LC
White-eyed Gull	Larus leucophthalmus	A	RB	LC
Pallas's Gull	Larus ichthyaetus	A	PV WV	LC
Mediterranean Gull	Larus melanocephalus	A	WV	LC
Sabine's Gull	Larus sabini	A	AV?	LC
Franklin's Gull	Larus pipixcan	A	AV	LC
Black-headed Gull	Larus ridibundus	A	PV WV	LC
Grey-headed Gull	Larus cirrocephalus	A	AV	LC
Slender-billed Gull	Larus genei	A	RB PV WV	LC
Audouin's Gull	Larus audouinii	A	PV	VU/LC
Mew Gull	Larus canus	A	WV	LC
Lesser Black-backed Gull	Larus fuscus	A	PV WV	LC
Caspian Gull	Larus cachinnans	A	PV	LC
Yellow-legged Gull	Larus michahellis	A	RB WV	LC
Armenian Gull	Larus armenicus	A	PV WV?	LC
Black-legged Kittiwake	Rissa tridactyla	A	(WV)	LC
Little Gull	Hydrocoloeus minutus	A	WV	LC
Sternidae (Terns)				
Gull-billed Tern	Gelochelidon nilotica	A	PV WV	LC
Caspian Tern	Hydroprogne caspia	A	RB PV WV	LC
Greater Crested Tern	Sterna bergii	A	RB? WV	LC
Lesser Crested Tern	Sterna bengalensis	A	MB PV	LC
Sandwich Tern	Sterna sandvicensis	A	PV WV	LC
Common Tern	Sterna hirundo	A	PV	LC
White-cheeked Tern	Sterna repressa	A	MB	LC
Bridled Tern	Onychoprion anaethetus	A	MB	LC
Little Tern	Sternula albifrons	A	MB PV	LC
Saunders's Tern	Sternula saundersi	A	PV MB?	LC
Whiskered Tern	Chlidonias hybrida	A	PV WV	LC
Black Tern	Chlidonias niger	A	PV WV	LC
White-winged Tern	Chlidonias leucopterus	A	PV (WV)	LC
Rynchopidae (Skimmers)				
African Skimmer	Rynchops flavirostris	A	FB? PV	NT
Pteroclidae (Sandgrouse)				
Lichtenstein's Sandgrouse	Pterocles lichtensteinii	A	RB	LC
Crowned Sandgrouse	Pterocles coronatus	A	RB	LC
Spotted Sandgrouse	Pterocles senegallus	A	RB	LC
Chestnut-bellied Sandgrouse	Pterocles exustus	A	FB (RB)	LC
Black-bellied Sandgrouse	Pterocles orientalis	A	(WV)	LC
Pin-tailed Sandgrouse	Pterocles alchata	A	AV	LC

Common name	Scientific name	Category	Status	IUCN
Columbidae (Pigeons and Doves)				
Rock Dove	Columba livia	A	RB	LC
Stock Dove	Columba oenas	A	WV	LC
Common Wood Pigeon	Columba palumbus	A	AV	LC
African Collared Dove	Streptopelia risoria	A	RB	LC
Mourning Collared Dove	Streptopelia decipiens	A	AV	LC
Eurasian Collared Dove	Streptopelia decaocto	A	RB	LC
European Turtle Dove	Streptopelia turtur	A	MB PV (WV)	LC
Oriental Turtle Dove	Streptopelia orientalis	A	AV	LC
Laughing Dove	Streptopelia senegalensis	A	RB	LC
Namaqua Dove	Oena capensis	A	RB? WV	LC
Bruce's Green Pigeon	Treron waalia	A	AV	LC
Psittacidae (Parrots)				
Rose-ringed Parakeet	Psittacula krameri	C	IB	LC
Cuculidae (Cuckoos)				
Great Spotted Cuckoo	Clamator glandarius	A	MB PV	LC
Common Cuckoo	Cuculus canorus	A	PV	LC
Senegal Coucal	Centropus senegalensis	A	RB	LC
Tytonidae (Barn Owls)				
Barn Owl	Tyto alba	A	RB	LC
Strigidae (Owls)				
Pallid Scops Owl	Otus brucei	B	AV	LC
Eurasian Scops Owl	Otus scops	A	PV	LC
Eurasian Eagle-Owl	Bubo bubo	A	RB	LC
Little Owl	Athene noctua	A	RB	LC
Hume's Owl	Strix butleri	A	RB	LC
Long-eared Owl	Asio otus	A	RB? PV WV	LC
Short-eared Owl	Asio flammeus	A	PV WV	LC
Caprimulgidae (Nightjars)				
Nubian Nightjar	Caprimulgus nubicus	GE	MB?	LC
European Nightjar	Caprimulgus europaeus	A	PV	LC
Egyptian Nightjar	Caprimulgus aegyptius	A	RB PV	LC
Apodidae (Swifts)				
Common Swift	Apus apus	A	PV	LC
Pallid Swift	Apus pallidus	A	RB MB PV	LC
Alpine Swift	Apus melba	A	PV (WV)	LC
Little Swift	Apus affinis	A	(PV)	LC
Alcedinidae (Kingfishers)				
White-throated Kingfisher	Halcyon smyrnensis	A	RB WV	LC
Common Kingfisher	Alcedo atthis	A	CB? WV	LC
Pied Kingfisher	Ceryle rudis	A	RB (WV)	LC
Meropidae (Bee-eaters)				
Green Bee-eater	Merops orientalis	A	RB	LC
Blue-cheeked Bee-eater	Merops persicus	A	MB PV	LC
European Bee-eater	Merops apiaster	A	MB PV	LC
Coraciidae (Rollers)				
European Roller	Coracias garrulus	A	PV	LC
Abyssinian Roller	Coracias abyssinicus	A	AV	LC
Broad-billed Roller	Eurystomus glaucurus	A	AV	LC
Upupidae (Hoopoes)				
Hoopoe	Upupa epops	A	RB PV	LC
Picidae (Woodpeckers)				
Eurasian Wryneck	Jynx torquilla	A	PV (WV)	LC

Common name	Scientific name	Category	Status	IUCN
Syrian Woodpecker	*Dendrocopos syriacus*	A	RB	LC
Alaudidae (Larks)				
Black-crowned Sparrow-Lark	*Eremopterix nigriceps*	A	RB	LC
Bar-tailed Lark	*Ammomanes cinctura*	A	RB	LC
Desert Lark	*Ammomanes deserti*	A	RB	LC
Greater Hoopoe-Lark	*Alaemon alaudipes*	A	RB	LC
Dupont's Lark	*Chersophilus duponti*	A	RB? FB	VU
Thick-billed Lark	*Ramphocoris clotbey*	A	(PV) (WV)	LC
Calandra Lark	*Melanocorypha calandra*	A	WV	LC
Bimaculated Lark	*Melanocorypha bimaculata*	A	PV	LC
Greater Short-toed Lark	*Calandrella brachydactyla*	A	PV (WV) CB	LC
Lesser Short-toed Lark	*Calandrella rufescens*	A	RB WV	LC
Crested Lark	*Galerida cristata*	A	RB	LC
Thekla Lark	*Galerida theklae*	A	RB?	LC
Woodlark	*Lullula arborea*	A	WV	LC
Oriental Skylark	*Alauda gulgula*	A	AV	LC
Eurasian Skylark	*Alauda arvensis*	A	WV	LC
Temminck's Lark	*Eremophila bilopha*	A	RB	LC
Hirundinidae (Swallows and Martins)				
Sand Martin	*Riparia riparia*	A	MB PV WV	LC
Banded Martin	*Riparia cincta*	A	AV	LC
Eurasian Crag Martin	*Ptyonoprogne rupestris*	A	(PV) (WV)	LC
Rock Martin	*Ptyonoprogne fuligula*	A	RB	LC
Barn Swallow	*Hirundo rustica*	A	RB PV WV	LC
Common House Martin	*Delichon urbicum*	A	PV (WV)	LC
Red-rumped Swallow	*Cecropis daurica*	A	PW (WV)	LC
Streak-throated Swallow	*Petrochelidon fluvicola*	A	AV	LC
Motacillidae (Wagtails and Pipits)				
Richard's Pipit	*Anthus richardi*	A	PV WV	LC
Tawny Pipit	*Anthus campestris*	A	PV WV	LC
Long-billed Pipit	*Anthus similis*	GE	AV	LC
Tree Pipit	*Anthus trivialis*	A	PV	LC
Meadow Pipit	*Anthus pratensis*	A	PV WV	LC
Red-throated Pipit	*Anthus cervinus*	A	PV WV	LC
Asian Buff-bellied Pipit	*Anthus rubescens japonicus*	A	AV	LC
Water Pipit	*Anthus spinoletta*	A	PV WV	LC
Yellow Wagtail	*Motacilla flava*	A	RB PV WV	LC
Citrine Wagtail	*Motacilla citreola*	A	AV?	LC
Grey Wagtail	*Motacilla cinerea*	A	PV WV	LC
White Wagtail	*Motacilla alba*	A	PV WV	LC
African Pied Wagtail	*Motacilla aguimp*	A	RB	LC
Pycnonotidae (Bulbuls)				
White-spectacled Bulbul	*Pycnonotus xanthopygos*	A	RB	LC
Common Bulbul	*Pycnonotus barbatus*	A	RB	LC
Bombycillidae (Waxwings and allies)				
Grey Hypocolius	*Hypocolius ampelinus*	A	AV	LC
Troglodytidae (Wrens)				
Winter Wren	*Troglodytes troglodytes*	A	AV?	LC
Prunellidae (Accentors)				
Dunnock	*Prunella modularis*	A	(WV)	LC
Turdidae (Thrushes, Chats and allies)				
Rufous-tailed Scrub Robin	*Cercotrichas galactotes*	A	MB PV (WV)	LC
Black Scrub Robin	*Cercotrichas podobe*	A	AV (PV)	LC

Common name	Scientific name	Category	Status	IUCN
European Robin	Erithacus rubecula	A	WV	LC
Thrush Nightingale	Luscinia luscinia	A	PV	LC
Common Nightingale	Luscinia megarhynchos	A	PV	LC
Bluethroat	Luscinia svecica	A	PV WV	LC
White-throated Robin	Irania gutturalis	A	AV	LC
Black Redstart	Phoenicurus ochruros	A	PV WV	LC
Common Redstart	Phoenicurus phoenicurus	A	PV (WV)	LC
Blackstart	Cercomela melanura	A	RB	LC
Whinchat	Saxicola rubetra	A	PV	LC
Pied Bush Chat	Saxicola caprata	A	AV	LC
European Stonechat	Saxicola rubicola	A	PV WV	LC
Eastern Stonechat	Saxicola maurus	A	PV?	LC
Isabelline Wheatear	Oenanthe isabellina	A	PV WV	LC
Northern Wheatear	Oenanthe oenanthe	A	PV (WV)	LC
Pied Wheatear	Oenanthe pleschanka	A	PV WV	LC
Cyprus Wheatear	Oenanthe cypriaca	A	PV WV	LC
Black-eared Wheatear	Oenanthe hispanica	A	PV (WV) MB?	LC
Desert Wheatear	Oenanthe deserti	A	RB PV WV	LC
Finsch's Wheatear	Oenanthe finschii	A	WV	LC
Red-rumped Wheatear	Oenanthe moesta	A	RB	LC
Kurdish Wheatear	Oenanthe xanthoprymna	A	WV	LC
Red-tailed Wheatear	Oenanthe chrysopygia	A	AV	LC
Mourning Wheatear	Oenanthe lugens (including warriae)	A	RB (WV)	LC
Hooded Wheatear	Oenanthe monacha	A	RB	LC
White-crowned Wheatear	Oenanthe leucopyga	A	RB	LC
Common Rock Thrush	Monticola saxatilis	A	PV (WV)	LC
Blue Rock Thrush	Monticola solitarius	A	CB? PV WV	LC
Ring Ouzel	Turdus torquatus	A	(WV)	LC
Common Blackbird	Turdus merula	A	RB WV	LC
Black-throated Thrush	Turdus atrogularis	A	AV	LC
Fieldfare	Turdus pilaris	A	(WV)	LC
Song Thrush	Turdus philomelos	A	WV	LC
Redwing	Turdus iliacus	A	(WV)	LC
Mistle Thrush	Turdus viscivorus	A	(WV)	LC
Sylviidae (Old World Warblers)				
Zitting Cisticola	Cisticola juncidis	A	RB	LC
Graceful Prinia	Prinia gracilis	A	RB	LC
Scrub Warbler	Scotocerca inquieta	A	RB	LC
River Warbler	Locustella fluviatilis	A	PV	LC
Savi's Warbler	Locustella luscinioides	A	PV WV?	LC
Western Olivaceous Warbler	Iduna opaca	A	PV	LC
Eastern Olivaceous Warbler	Iduna pallida	A	MB PV (WV?)	LC
Moustached Warbler	Acrocephalus melanopogon	A	PV WV?	LC
Sedge Warbler	Acrocephalus schoenobaenus	A	PV (WV)	LC
Marsh Warbler	Acrocephalus palustris	A	PV	LC
Eurasian Reed Warbler	Acrocephalus scirpaceus	A	MB? PV (WV)	LC
Clamorous Reed Warbler	Acrocephalus stentoreus	A	RB	LC
Great Reed Warbler	Acrocephalus arundinaceus	A	PV	LC
Upcher's Warbler	Hippolais languida	A	PV?	LC
Olive-tree Warbler	Hippolais olivetorum	A	PV	LC
Icterine Warbler	Hippolais icterina	A	PV (WV)	LC
Spectacled Warbler	Sylvia conspicillata	A	RB? WV	LC
Subalpine Warbler	Sylvia cantillans	A	PV WV	LC

Common name	Scientific name	Category	Status	IUCN
Menetries's Warbler	*Sylvia mystacea*	A	(PV) (WV)	LC
Sardinian Warbler	*Sylvia melanocephala*	A	RB PV WV	LC
Cyprus Warbler	*Sylvia melanothorax*	A	AV	LC
Rüppell's Warbler	*Sylvia rueppelli*	A	PV (WV)	LC
Asian Desert Warbler	*Sylvia nana*	A	PV WV	LC
Arabian Warbler	*Sylvia leucomelaena*	A	RB	LC
Eastern Orphean Warbler	*Sylvia crassirostris*	A	PV (WV)	LC
Barred Warbler	*Sylvia nisoria*	A	PV	LC
Lesser Whitethroat	*Sylvia curruca*	A	PV WV	LC
Common Whitethroat	*Sylvia communis*	A	PV	LC
Garden Warbler	*Sylvia borin*	A	PV WV?	LC
Eurasian Blackcap	*Sylvia atricapilla*	A	PV WV	LC
Yellow-browed Warbler	*Phylloscopus inornatus*	A	(PV)	LC
Dusky Warbler	*Phylloscopus fuscatus*	A	AV	LC
Western Bonelli's Warbler	*Phylloscopus bonelli*	A	PV	LC
Eastern Bonelli's Warbler	*Phylloscopus orientalis*	A	PV	LC
Wood Warbler	*Phylloscopus sibilatrix*	A	PV	LC
Common Chiffchaff	*Phylloscopus collybita*	A	PV WV	LC
Willow Warbler	*Phylloscopus trochilus*	A	PV (WV)	LC
Goldcrest	*Regulus regulus*	A	(WV)	LC
Common Firecrest	*Regulus ignicapilla*	A	AV	LC
Muscicapidae (Old World Flycatchers)				
Spotted Flycatcher	*Muscicapa striata*	A	PV (WV)	LC
Red-breasted Flycatcher	*Ficedula parva*	A	PV (WV)	LC
Semicollared Flycatcher	*Ficedula semitorquata*	A	PV	LC
Collared Flycatcher	*Ficedula albicollis*	A	PV	LC
European Pied Flycatcher	*Ficedula hypoleuca*	A	PV	LC
Timaliidae (Babblers and allies)				
Bearded Reedling	*Panurus biarmicus*	A	AV	LC
Arabian Babbler	*Turdoides squamiceps*	A	RB	LC
Fulvous Babbler	*Turdoides fulva*	A	RB	LC
Paridae (Tits)				
Great Tit	*Parus major*	A	RB	LC
Remizidae (Penduline Tits)				
Eurasian Penduline Tit	*Remiz pendulinus*	A	WV	LC
Nectariniidae (Sunbirds)				
Nile Valley Sunbird	*Anthreptes metallicus*	A	RB	LC
Shining Sunbird	*Nectarinia habessinica*	GE	RB	LC
Palestine Sunbird	*Nectarinia osea*	A	RB	LC
Oriolidae (Old World Orioles)				
Eurasian Golden Oriole	*Oriolus oriolus*	A	PV	LC
Laniidae (Shrikes)				
Rosy-patched Shrike	*Rhodophoneus cruentus*	GE	RB	LC
Daurian Shrike	*Lanius isabellinus*	A	(PV)	LC
Red-backed Shrike	*Lanius collurio*	A	PV (WV)	LC
Lesser Grey Shrike	*Lanius minor*	A	PV	LC
Southern Grey Shrike	*Lanius meridionalis*	A	RB WV	LC
Woodchat Shrike	*Lanius senator*	A	PV	LC
Masked Shrike	*Lanius nubicus*	A	PV	LC
Corvidae (Crows and Ravens)				
House Crow	*Corvus splendens*	C	IB	LC
Rook	*Corvus frugilegus*	A	(WV)	LC
Carrion Crow	*Corvus corone*	A	RB	LC

Common name	Scientific name	Category	Status	IUCN
Pied Crow	Corvus albus	A	AV	LC
Brown-necked Raven	Corvus ruficollis	A	RB	LC
Northern Raven	Corvus corax	A	RB	LC
Fan-tailed Raven	Corvus rhipidurus	A	RB	LC
Sturnidae (Starlings)				
Tristram's Starling	Onychognathus tristramii	A	RB	LC
Common Starling	Sturnus vulgaris	A	WV	LC
Rosy Starling	Pastor roseus	A	(PV)	LC
Common Myna	Acridotheres tristis	C	(RB)	LC
Passeridae (Sparrows and allies)				
House Sparrow	Passer domesticus	A	RB	LC
Spanish Sparrow	Passer hispaniolensis	A	PV WV	LC
Dead Sea Sparrow	Passer moabiticus	A	AV?	LC
Desert Sparrow	Passer simplex	A	AV	LC
Eurasian Tree Sparrow	Passer montanus	A	AV	LC
Sudan Golden Sparrow	Passer luteus	GE	MB?	LC
Pale Rockfinch	Carpospiza brachydactyla	A	(PV)	LC
Yellow-throated Sparrow	Gymnoris xanthocollis	A	AV	LC
Ploceidae (Weavers)				
Village Weaver	Ploceus cucullatus	A	AV?	LC
Streaked Weaver	Ploceus manyar	C	IB	LC
Estrilidae (Avadavats and Mannikins)				
Red Avadavat	Amandava amandava	C	IB	LC
Indian Silverbill	Euodice malabarica	C	IB?	LC
African Silverbill	Euodice cantans	GE	RB?	LC
Fringillidae (Finches)				
Common Chaffinch	Fringilla coelebs	A	WV	LC
Brambling	Fringilla montifringilla	A	WV	LC
Red-fronted Serin	Serinus pusillus	A	AV	LC
European Serin	Serinus serinus	A	RB? WV	LC
Syrian Serin	Serinus syriacus	A	WV	VU
European Greenfinch	Carduelis chloris	A	RB WV	LC
European Goldfinch	Carduelis carduelis	A	RB WV	LC
Eurasian Siskin	Carduelis spinus	A	WV	LC
Common Linnet	Carduelis cannabina	A	WV	LC
Trumpeter Finch	Bucanetes githagineus	A	RB	LC
Common Rosefinch	Carpodacus erythrinus	A	(PV)	LC
Sinai Rosefinch	Carpodacus synoicus	A	RB	LC
Hawfinch	Coccothraustes coccothraustes	A	WV	LC
Emberizidae (Buntings)				
Cirl Bunting	Emberiza cirlus	B	AV	LC
Striolated Bunting	Emberiza striolata	A	RB	LC
Cinereous Bunting	Emberiza cineracea	A	AV	LC
Ortolan Bunting	Emberiza hortulana	A	PV (WV)	LC
Grey-necked Bunting	Emberiza buchanani	A	AV	LC
Cretzschmar's Bunting	Emberiza caesia	A	PV WV?	LC
Rustic Bunting	Emberiza rustica	A	AV	LC
Little Bunting	Emberiza pusilla	A	AV	LC
Yellow-breasted Bunting	Emberiza aureola	A	AV	VU
Common Reed Bunting	Emberiza schoeniclus	A	AV	LC
Red-headed Bunting	Emberiza bruniceps	A	AV	LC
Black-headed Bunting	Emberiza melanocephala	A	PV	LC
Corn Bunting	Emberiza calandra	A	PV WV	LC

■ References & Further Reading ■

References
A key source of information on the birds of Egypt and the Middle East is the Ornithological Society of the Middle East, the Caucasus and Central Asia (OSME). OSME's journal, *Sandgrouse*, is published twice a year, and its website is www.osme.org.

The Egyptian Ornithological Rarities Committee is the body concerned with recording records of new and rare species in Egypt. Reports can be made through its website at the Egyptian Ornithological Rarities Committee (chn-france.org).

Further Reading
The following list includes books containing in-depth identification of groups of birds, guides to individual countries within the Region, as well as titles of more general interest.

Alstrom, Per & Mild, Krister. 2003. *Pipits and Wagtails*. Helm Identification Guides, London.

Aly, Dina & Khalil, Rafik. 2011. *Wildlife in South Sinai*. Dina Aly and Rafik Khalil, Cairo.

Baha El Din, Sherif M. 1999. *Directory of Important Bird Areas in Egypt*. Birdlife International, Cambridge.

Beaman, Mark & Madge, Steve. 1998. *The Handbook of Bird Identification for Europe and the Western Palearctic*. Christopher Helm, A&C Black, London.

Cheke, Robert A., Mann, Clive F. & Allen, Richard. 2001. *Sunbirds*. Helm Identification Guides, London.

Eriksen, Hanne & Eriksen, Jens. 2010. *Common Birds in Oman*. 2nd edn. Al Roya Publishing, Muscat.

Evans, M. I. 1994. *Important Bird Areas in the Middle East*. Birdlife Conservation Series No. 2, Birdlife International, Cambridge.

Goodman, Steven M. & Meininger, Peter L. (eds). 1989. *The Birds of Egypt*. Oxford University Press, Oxford.

Hoath, Richard 2009. *A Field Guide to the Mammals of Egypt*. 2nd edn. AUC Press, Cairo.

Hollom, P. A. D., et al. 1988. *Birds of the Middle East and North Africa*. T & A D Poyser, Calton.

Houlihan, Patrick F. 1988. *The Birds of Ancient Egypt*. AUC Press, Cairo.

Jiguet, Frédéric & Audevard, Aurelien. 2017. *Birds of Europe, North Africa and the Middle East*. Princeton University Press, Princeton.

Jonsson, L. 1992. *Birds of Europe with North Africa and the Middle East*. Christopher Helm, London.

Meininger, Peter L. & Atta, Gamil A. M. (eds). 1990. *Ornithological Studies in Egyptian Wetlands 1989/90*. FORE-report 94-01, WIWO-report Nr 40, Vissengen/Zeist.

Olsen, Klaus M. & Larsson, Hans. 2007. *Gulls of Europe, Asia and North America*. Helm Identification Guides, London.

Porter, Richard & Aspinall, Simon. 2010. *Birds of the Middle East*. 2nd edn. Helm Field Guides, Christopher Helm, London.

Redman, Nigel, Stevenson, Terry & Fanshawe, John. 2009. *Birds of the Horn of Africa; Ethiopia, Eritrea, Djibouti, Somalia and Socotra*. Princeton University Press, Princeton.

■ References & Further Reading ■

Robinson, Dave & Chapman, Adrian. 1992. *The Birds of Southern Arabia*. Motivate Publishing, Exxon, Dubai.

Rosair, David & Cotteridge, David. 1995. *Photographic Guide to the Waders of the World*. Hamlyn, London.

Sargeant, Dave E., Eriksen, Hanne & Eriksen, Jens. 2008. *Birdwatching Guide to Oman*. 2nd edn. Al Roya Publishing, Muscat.

Shirihai, Hadoram. *The Birds of Israel*. Princeton University Press, Princeton.

Sterry, Paul. 2004. *Birds of the Mediterranean: A Photographic Guide*. Yale University Press, New Haven.

Stevenson, T. & Fanshawe, J. 2006. *Birds of East Africa*. Helm Field Guides, Christopher Helm, London.

Acknowledgements

Any guide of this type builds on the works that have gone before it. I acknowledge those works in 'References and Further Reading', and have had the privilege of having met and benefited from a number of those who have authored these works. I would particularly like to thank, for their expertise and experience, the members of the Egyptian Ornithological Rarities Committee (EORC) with whom I have served over the last ten years. The current members are Sherif Baha El Din, Mohamed Habib, Andrea Corso, Pierre André Crochet, Arnoud van den Berg, Manuel Schweizer, Ahmed Waheed, Frédéric Jiguet and Lukasz Lawicki but I would also pay tribute to all former members. Mindy Baha El Din was instrumental in setting up this committee, and also influential have been Andrew Grieve, Ahmed Riad and Mary Megalli. Special appreciation must be given to the EORC for the checklist (pages 159–169).

I would also like to acknowledge all the officers past and present at the Ornithological Society of the Middle East (OSME) for providing such a constant forum for the exchange of information, data and discussion over many years. I have enjoyed many of their annual meetings in London and Thetford, and most recently by Zoom over recent years. Those conferences provide evidence of the depth and scope of interest in the Region's birds.

I would like to pay especial thanks to my peer reviewers Sherif Baha El Din, Andy Main and Dina Aly. While I greatly appreciate their reviews, any shortfalls are my own. Thanks also to Watter Al-Bahry. For support in this project I thank especially Andrew Humphreys and Nigel Fletcher-Jones.

At John Beaufoy Publishing I would like to thank Rosemary Wilkinson and Krystyna Mayer for all their work and assistance, and at The AUC Press Nadia Naqib and Neil Hewison for their advice and additional editing.

For their support over the time working on this book I would especially like to thank Marion Pearson, Mark Pearson, Leigh Devenish, Rafik Khalil, Liz Sear, Arthur Bos, Menna Megahed, Hana Heiba, Gretchen McCullough, Jeanne Arnold, Kathleen Saville, Salima Ikram, Dina Ratef, Melanie Carter and Peter Barsoum.

Finally I would like to very gratefully acknowledge Jonathan Hoath for his unwavering and much appreciated support and Pam Hoath for opening her home to an author's 'hub' during a difficult lockdown time. This book would not have been possible without them.